GW00833035

PLAY IDEAS
FOR YOU & YOUR CHILD

Ray Gibson and Jenny Tyler

Illustrated by Simone Abel, Sue Stitt
and Graham Round

Designed by Carol Law

Edited by Robyn Gee

Contents

1 Playdough
33 Paperplay
65 Odds and Ends
97 Kitchen Fun

First published in 1990 by Usborne Publishing Ltd., Usborne House, 83-85 Saffron Hill, London EC1N 8RT, England. Copyright © 1990 Usborne Publishing Ltd. The name Usborne and the device ⬱ are Trade Marks of Usborne Publishing Ltd. All rights reserved. No part of this publication may be reproduced, stored in any form or by any means, mechanical, electronic, photocopying, recording, or otherwise without the prior permission of the publisher. Printed in Belgium.

PLAYDOUGH

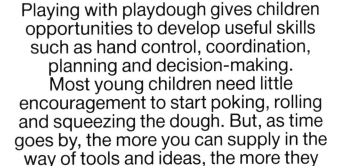

Playing with playdough gives children
opportunities to develop useful skills
such as hand control, coordination,
planning and decision-making.
Most young children need little
encouragement to start poking, rolling
and squeezing the dough. But, as time
goes by, the more you can supply in the
way of tools and ideas, the more they
will learn from it. This book is designed
to give you some starting points.

Caterpillar on a leaf

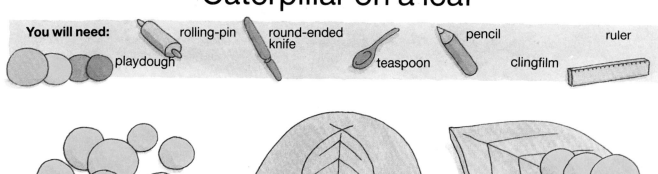

You will need: rolling-pin · round-ended knife · pencil · ruler · playdough · teaspoon · clingfilm

Roll seven or eight balls of different sizes.

Roll out some green dough on clingfilm. Using a knife, cut out a leaf shape and mark veins on it.

Position the balls in a row on the leaf, starting with the biggest and ending with the smallest.

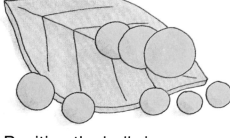

Roll two small balls of dough for eyes. Press them onto the head with the pointed end of a pencil. Make two pencil holes for nostrils and mark in the mouth with the end of a teaspoon.

Other ideas

Ladybird
Flatten a ball of dough, then press the side of a ruler across the centre.

Press on small flattened balls for spots and eyes.

Roll two small antennae.

Attach head.

Poke small white balls into centre of each eye with a pencil point.

Mark mouth with side of spoon.

Mark in nostrils with a pencil point.

Bee
Flatten three balls of dough and press them together. Fix on a round head and a pointed tail.

Press on eyes with a pencil point.

Add two pear-shaped wings.

Mark nostrils and mouth.

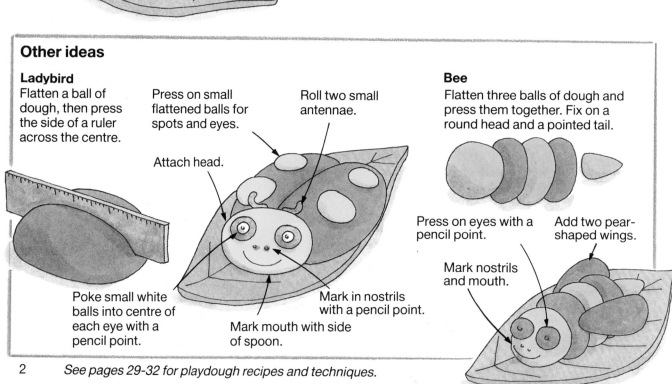

See pages 29-32 for playdough recipes and techniques.

Snowman by a pond

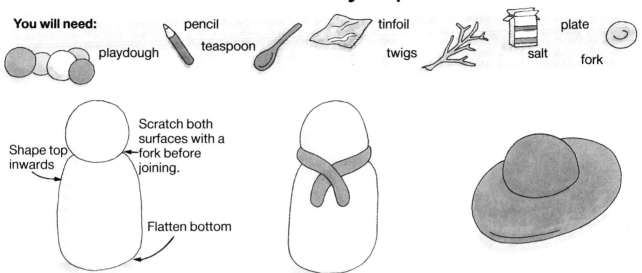

You will need: playdough, pencil, teaspoon, tinfoil, twigs, salt, plate, fork

Shape top inwards

Scratch both surfaces with a fork before joining.

Flatten bottom

Roll a thick sausage of white dough for the body and a small ball for the head. Join them together.

Roll a long thin sausage for a scarf and wrap it around the snowman's neck.

To make a hat, roll a small ball and flatten it. Then roll another ball and press it onto the flattened one.

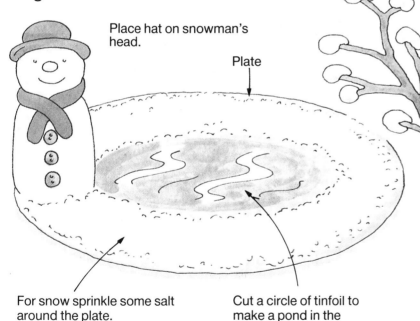

Place hat on snowman's head.

Plate

For snow sprinkle some salt around the plate.

Cut a circle of tinfoil to make a pond in the centre.

Mark in the eyes with a pencil and the mouth with a teaspoon and roll a tiny ball for the nose. Roll three small balls for the buttons and poke each one twice with a pencil. Place the snowman on the plate.

Other ideas to try

Tree
Push a twig into a ball of dough. Roll some tiny balls of white dough and stick them on the ends of the twig. Place it by the pond.

Duck
Roll two small balls for the body and head and join them together.

Roll a tiny sausage for the beak. Pinch out a tail. Put the duck on the pond.

3

Pigs in a pen

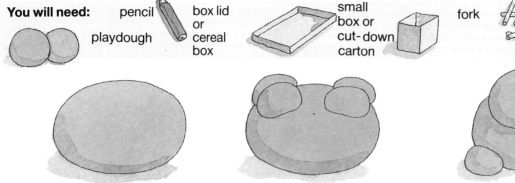

You will need: pencil   box lid or cereal box   playdough   small box or cut-down carton   fork   drinking straws

Roll a ball of dough for the body.

Roll four small balls for the feet. Press them on to the body.

Roll a ball for the head. Join the head to the body.

← Scratch surfaces with fork to join (see page 32).

Flatten and pinch ears. Press on to head.

Press on snout.

Roll two small balls for the ears and one for the snout.

Roll a thin sausage for the tail.

Mark holes for the eyes and snout with a pencil.

Pig pen and cabbages

You could make several pigs and then make a pen for them.

Cut a doorway in the small box, or cut-down carton. Put it upside down inside the box lid to make a shed.

Cut up some paper or drinking straws for the pigs to lie on.

Make some tiny baby pigs too.

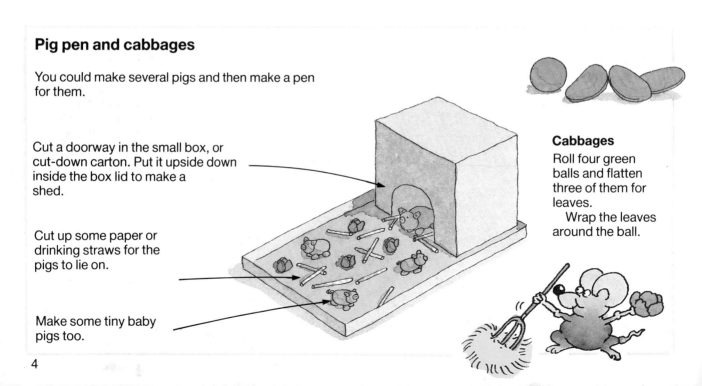

Cabbages
Roll four green balls and flatten three of them for leaves.
    Wrap the leaves around the ball.

Sheep in a field

You will need: pencil — playdough — fork and round-ended knife — box lid or cereal box — sieve or garlic press — paint

Roll a fat sausage of dough for the body.

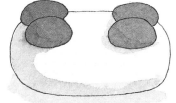

Roll four small balls for the feet and press them on.

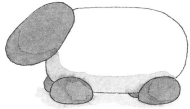

Roll a fat sausage for the head and fix it to the body.

Roll two smaller sausages for the ears.

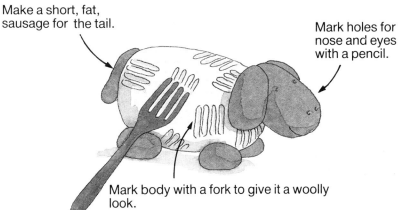

Make a short, fat, sausage for the tail.

Mark holes for nose and eyes with a pencil.

Mark body with a fork to give it a woolly look.

Field, flowers and bushes

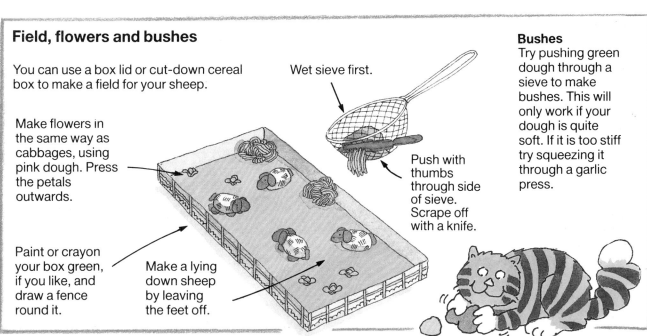

You can use a box lid or cut-down cereal box to make a field for your sheep.

Make flowers in the same way as cabbages, using pink dough. Press the petals outwards.

Paint or crayon your box green, if you like, and draw a fence round it.

Make a lying down sheep by leaving the feet off.

Wet sieve first.

Push with thumbs through side of sieve. Scrape off with a knife.

Bushes
Try pushing green dough through a sieve to make bushes. This will only work if your dough is quite soft. If it is too stiff try squeezing it through a garlic press.

Cat on a cushion

You will need: pencil, rolling-pin, felt-tip pen, straw, round-ended knife, saltdough*, lightly oiled baking tray, paint, clingfilm

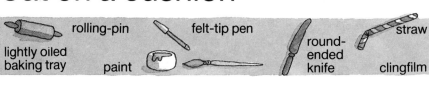

Mark in the eyes with a pencil point.

Flatten the bottom.

Roll a ball of dough for the body. Press in a piece of straw. Attach a smaller ball for the head.

Roll a thin sausage of dough for the collar and wrap it around the neck.

Roll a thicker sausage for the tail. Press it on and wrap it round. Pinch out the ears.

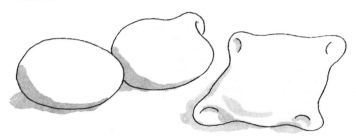

Mark in the face with felt-tip pen.

Roll a ball of dough and flatten it in the palm of your hand.
    Pinch out the sides to make four corners. Sit the cat on the cushion.

Bake in the oven before painting.*

Cat on a mat and other ideas

Roll out some dough on clingfilm and cut an oblong shape.

Press patterns in it with a straw and decorate the edges with a knife.

Lay the body of the cat on the mat before adding the head and tail.

A bowl for your cat
Roll a small ball and press the end of a pencil into it.

Fish on a plate
Cut a fish shape from a flat piece of dough. Flatten a ball of dough for the plate.

*To find out how to make, bake and decorate saltdough, see page 30.

Sausage dog

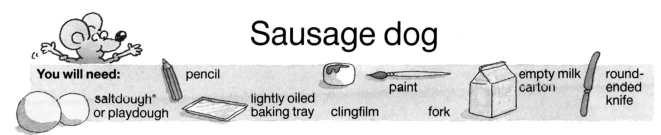

You will need: pencil, saltdough* or playdough, lightly oiled baking tray, paint, clingfilm, fork, empty milk carton, round-ended knife

Scratch surfaces with fork to join (see page 5)

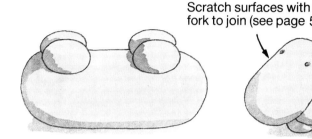
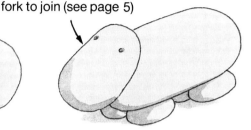

Roll a long, fat sausage of dough for the body and press on four small balls for feet.

Roll a short, fat sausage for the head. Join it to the body. Mark in the eyes with a pencil.

Roll two small sausages and flatten them to make ears. Join them to the top of the head.

Roll a small sausage for the tail and a tiny ball of dough for the nose. Press them on.

Mark in the whiskers with a pencil point and the mouth with a teaspoon. Bake your dog and then paint it.

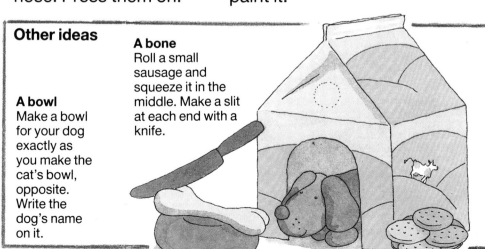

Other ideas

A bowl
Make a bowl for your dog exactly as you make the cat's bowl, opposite. Write the dog's name on it.

A bone
Roll a small sausage and squeeze it in the middle. Make a slit at each end with a knife.

A kennel
Cut down a clean milk carton. Cut out a doorway, making sure your dog can fit through it.

Dog biscuits
Flatten lots of small balls of dough, then prick them with a pencil point.

*To find out how to make, bake and decorate saltdough, see page 30.

7

Baby in a matchbox

You will need: saltdough* pencil empty matchbox rolling-pin paint kitchen roll felt-tip pen cotton wool clingfilm glue wool scissors

Scratch surfaces to join.

Roll a small ball for the head and a sausage for the body. Join them together.

Mark in the eyes with a pencil. Roll a tiny ball for the nose.

For the blanket, roll out a piece of dough on clingfilm. Make markings with a pencil point.

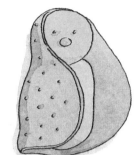

Peel off the clingfilm, turn the blanket over and wrap it round the baby.

Bake and then paint the baby. Mark on its mouth with a felt-tip pen.

Cut three small pieces of kitchen roll to make a sheet, pillow and blanket.
   Place the sheet and pillow in the matchbox. Put the baby in and lay the blanket over the baby.

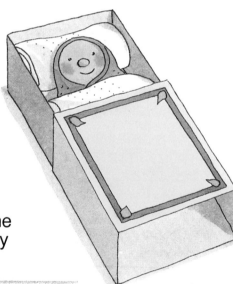

Other things to try

Baby's bottle
Roll a thin sausage for the bottle. Squash a small ball and place it on top. Roll a tiny sausage for the teat. Bake and paint.

Mouse in a matchbox
Roll a small ball of dough. Pinch out a nose. Stick a tiny ball on the end.

Flatten two balls for ears and press them on with the end of a pencil. Bake and

cotton wool

paint, then glue on a wool tail.

*To find out how to make, bake and decorate saltdough, see page 30.

Snail family

You will need: 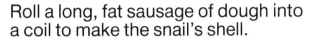 pencil   twigs   playdough   teaspoon   fork

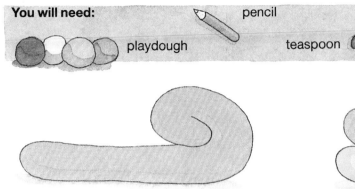

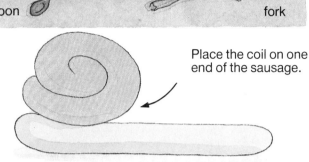

Place the coil on one end of the sausage.

Roll a long, fat sausage of dough into a coil to make the snail's shell.

Roll a shorter sausage and place the coil on top of it.

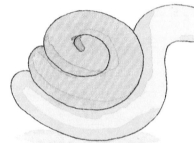

Bend up the ends and press to the coil. Bend the longer end forward to make a head.

Press on two balls for eyes with a pencil. Mark in the mouth with a teaspoon.

Decorate your snail by pressing little pieces of dough of another colour all over him.
   Make a family of snails of various sizes.

Ideas for snakes

To make snakes roll long sausages of dough. Mark in their eyes with a pencil and mouths with a teaspoon.

Snakes in a basket

For the base of the basket, flatten a ball of dough.

Roll a long thin sausage. Press one end to the edge of the base and coil around.

You may have to make another sausage. Simply press it on where the first one ended and continue coiling.

Arrange some snakes in your basket.

Snake in a tree
Wind your snake around a twig.

These look good on window-ledges.

Hedgehog

You will need: playdough   beads, buttons or lentils   round-ended knife   pieces of spaghetti   pencil   children's scissors

Roll a ball of dough
and pinch out a snout.

Add four balls of dough
for feet.

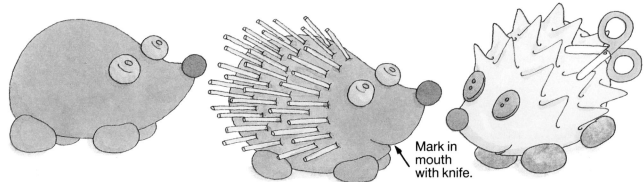

Mark in
mouth
with knife.

Add lentils, beads or
buttons for eyes and a
tiny ball of dough for
the nose.

Starting from the front, press in spaghetti "quills".
Or you can snip the dough with scissors for a
spiky effect.

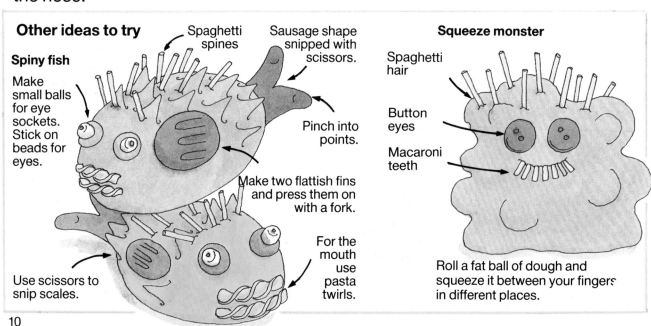

Other ideas to try

Spaghetti spines

Sausage shape snipped with scissors.

Squeeze monster

Spiny fish

Make
small balls
for eye
sockets.
Stick on
beads for
eyes.

Pinch into
points.

Make two flattish fins
and press them on
with a fork.

Use scissors to
snip scales.

For the
mouth
use
pasta
twirls.

Spaghetti
hair

Button
eyes

Macaroni
teeth

Roll a fat ball of dough and
squeeze it between your fingers
in different places.

Dragon

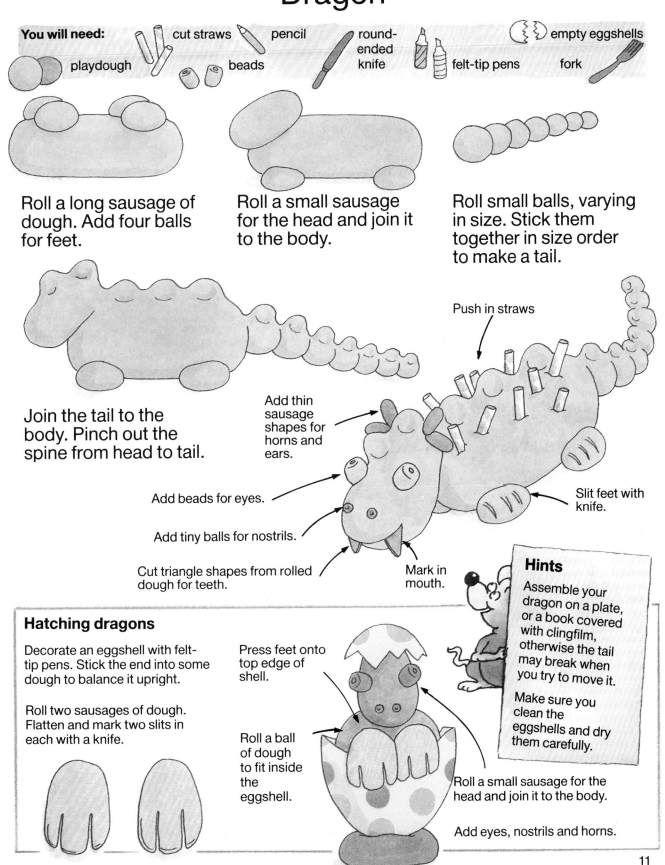

You will need: cut straws, pencil, round-ended knife, felt-tip pens, empty eggshells, playdough, beads, fork

Roll a long sausage of dough. Add four balls for feet.

Roll a small sausage for the head and join it to the body.

Roll small balls, varying in size. Stick them together in size order to make a tail.

Join the tail to the body. Pinch out the spine from head to tail.

Add thin sausage shapes for horns and ears.

Push in straws

Add beads for eyes.

Add tiny balls for nostrils.

Cut triangle shapes from rolled dough for teeth.

Mark in mouth.

Slit feet with knife.

Hints

Assemble your dragon on a plate, or a book covered with clingfilm, otherwise the tail may break when you try to move it.

Make sure you clean the eggshells and dry them carefully.

Hatching dragons

Decorate an eggshell with felt-tip pens. Stick the end into some dough to balance it upright.

Roll two sausages of dough. Flatten and mark two slits in each with a knife.

Press feet onto top edge of shell.

Roll a ball of dough to fit inside the eggshell.

Roll a small sausage for the head and join it to the body.

Add eyes, nostrils and horns.

11

Jewellery

You will need:
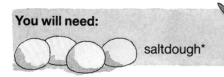
saltdough*
knitting needle
scone cutters
paint
wool
pasta shapes
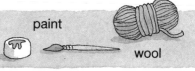

Bead necklace

Roll a sausage and cut it into pieces.

Poke the knitting needle through their centres.

Put the beads upright on a baking tray and bake them.

Paint the beads in bright colours.

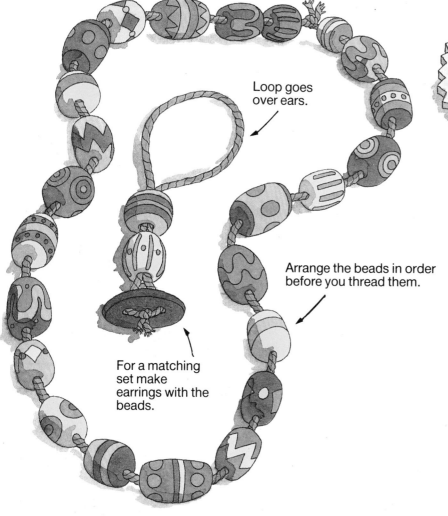

Loop goes over ears.

Arrange the beads in order before you thread them.

For a matching set make earrings with the beads.

Thread the beads, using wool, shoelaces or ribbon

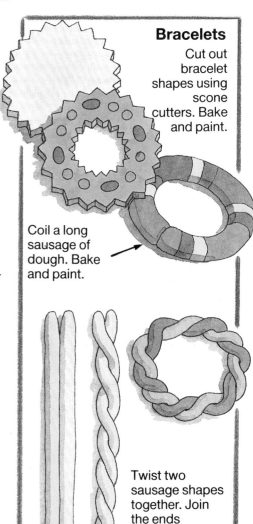

Bracelets

Cut out bracelet shapes using scone cutters. Bake and paint.

Coil a long sausage of dough. Bake and paint.

Twist two sausage shapes together. Join the ends together. Bake and paint.

12

*To find out how to make, bake and decorate saltdough, see page 30.

 lightly-oiled baking tray

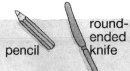 pencil

round-ended knife

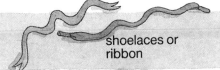 shoelaces or ribbon

plaster

 safety pin

Teddy earrings

Roll a small ball of dough and flatten for the teddy's head.

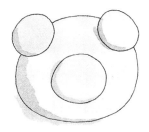

Flatten three smaller balls for ears and nose. Join them to the head.

Mark the eyes with a pencil and make a hole at the top.

Tie a ribbon through the hole.

Bake and paint the earring. Mark in a nose and mouth with felt-tip pens.

Hints

Take care to make the holes big enough as the dough will shrink when baked.

For small things like this bake for only 10 to 15 minutes.

Brooches and other earring ideas

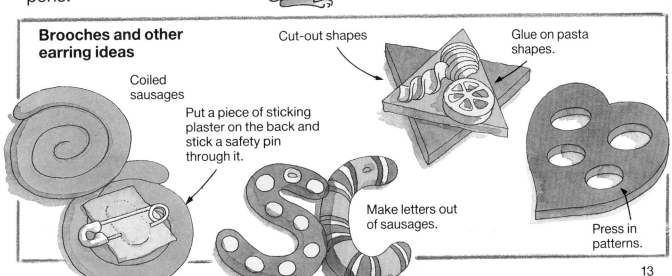

Coiled sausages

Cut-out shapes

Glue on pasta shapes.

Put a piece of sticking plaster on the back and stick a safety pin through it.

Make letters out of sausages.

Press in patterns.

13

Playdough people

You will need: pencil round-ended knife garlic press pen top  rolling-pin

 playdough teaspoon rolling-pin

Man

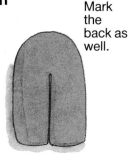

Mark the back as well.

Roll a long, thick sausage. Mark his legs by pressing a knife lightly along half his length.

Roll two sausage-shaped arms and small balls for hands. Add two balls for his feet.

Add a tiny ball for the nose.

Tiny balls poked in with pencil.

Roll a ball for his head. Mark in his eyes with a pencil and his mouth with a teaspoon.

Thin sausage for belt.

Press buckle on with used match end.

For his hair, cut tiny strips of dough, or press some dough through a garlic press.

Woman

See hint on joining pieces together.

Roll a thick sausage for her lower body. Add a smaller shape for her chest.

Add her head, arms and feet, as above, and mark in her face.

Buttons pressed on with pencil.

Thin sausage for belt.

Decorate skirt with a pen top.

Give her some hair, then cut a triangle from rolled dough as a scarf.

Hints

Secure head to body by pushing in a piece of straw.

Try putting the arms in different positions, or carefully bending the legs, so that your people can sit down.

Other ideas to try

Bags and baskets
For a basket, poke in the centre of a ball of dough with the end of a pencil. For the bag flatten a ball of dough. Make the handles from thin sausages.

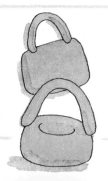

Hats
Flatten balls of dough with a finger. Roll small balls and place on top, then squash into shape.

14

Child in bed

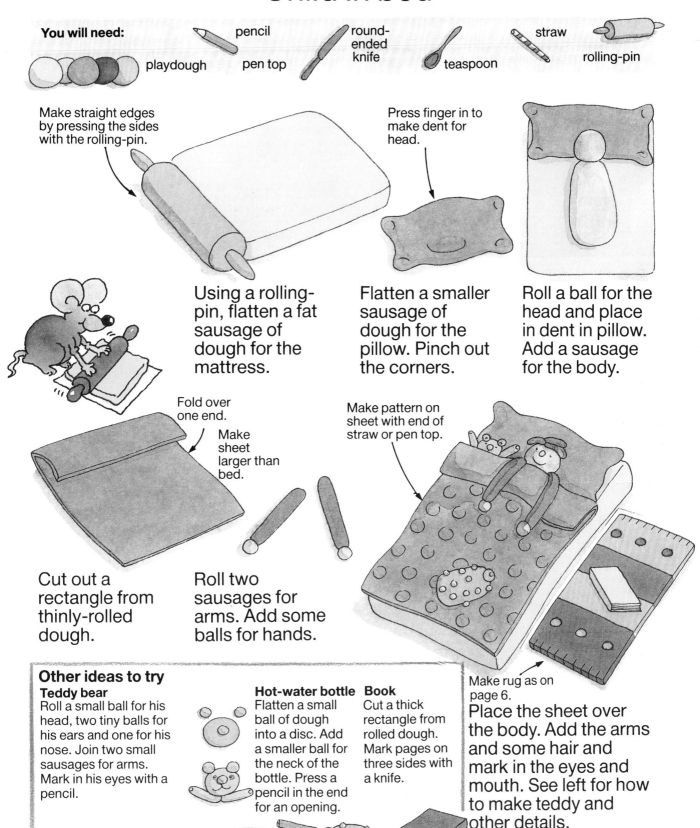

You will need:
playdough — pencil — pen top — round-ended knife — teaspoon — straw — rolling-pin

Make straight edges by pressing the sides with the rolling-pin.

Using a rolling-pin, flatten a fat sausage of dough for the mattress.

Press finger in to make dent for head.

Flatten a smaller sausage of dough for the pillow. Pinch out the corners.

Roll a ball for the head and place in dent in pillow. Add a sausage for the body.

Fold over one end.

Make sheet larger than bed.

Cut out a rectangle from thinly-rolled dough.

Roll two sausages for arms. Add some balls for hands.

Make pattern on sheet with end of straw or pen top.

Make rug as on page 6.

Place the sheet over the body. Add the arms and some hair and mark in the eyes and mouth. See left for how to make teddy and other details.

Other ideas to try
Teddy bear
Roll a small ball for his head, two tiny balls for his ears and one for his nose. Join two small sausages for arms. Mark in his eyes with a pencil.

Hot-water bottle
Flatten a small ball of dough into a disc. Add a smaller ball for the neck of the bottle. Press a pencil in the end for an opening.

Book
Cut a thick rectangle from rolled dough. Mark pages on three sides with a knife.

15

Special occasions

You will need:

playdough and saltdough*

straw

rolling-pin

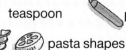

teaspoon

pasta shapes

pencil

eggs

A Christmas nativity scene

Mary

Roll a short, fat sausage for her body, so she will look as if she is kneeling.

Add arms, hands and a head. Mark in her mouth and eyes. Flatten a ball of dough for her cloak.

Drape the cloak over her head and body, so it lies in folds behind her.

Joseph and shepherd

Cut down a straw for a stick.

Give them taller bodies. For the shepherd roll a long, thin headband.

For gifts cut cubes from thickly-rolled dough and decorate with pasta shapes.

To make sheep see page 5.

Crib

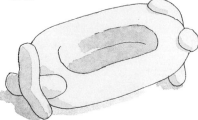

Roll a fat sausage. Press a bent finger firmly into the centre. Roll four thin sausages for crosses at each end.

Three kings

You can add a feather.

Give them brightly coloured cloaks. Make headbands by joining balls of dough, or twisting sausages.

Make the baby Jesus as shown on page 8. Put him in the crib.

16

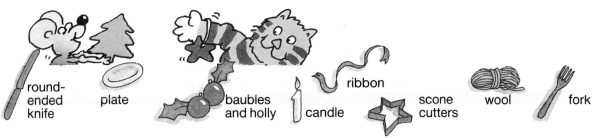

round-ended knife   plate   baubles and holly   candle   ribbon   scone cutters   wool   fork

Christmas log candle-holder

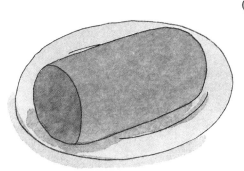

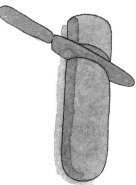

Roll a fat, long sausage for the log. Cut each end with a knife and put on a plate.

Roll a small "branch". Cut one end off diagonally, before joining it to the log.

Scratch in a bark pattern with a fork and mark the rings at each end with a teaspoon.

Don't use ribbon, it might catch fire.

Push a candle firmly into the log and then decorate it with baubles and holly.

Saltdough tree shapes

Roll dough out thinly. Cut out shapes with biscuit cutters or a round-ended knife. Poke a hole in each one. Bake and paint*.

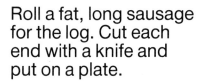

Easter ideas

Egg faces

Roll a ball of dough and stand it on a plate. Press a hard-boiled egg into it, pointed end down. Add hair, faces and hats.

Hen on a nest

Make a hen by pressing together the parts shown above.

Make a disc of dough. Roll lots of thin sausages. Twist them together, then press them round the disc to form the sides.

Roll some coloured eggs to put in the nest.

*To find out how to make, bake and decorate saltdough, see page 30.

17

Hallowe'en party decorations

You will need:

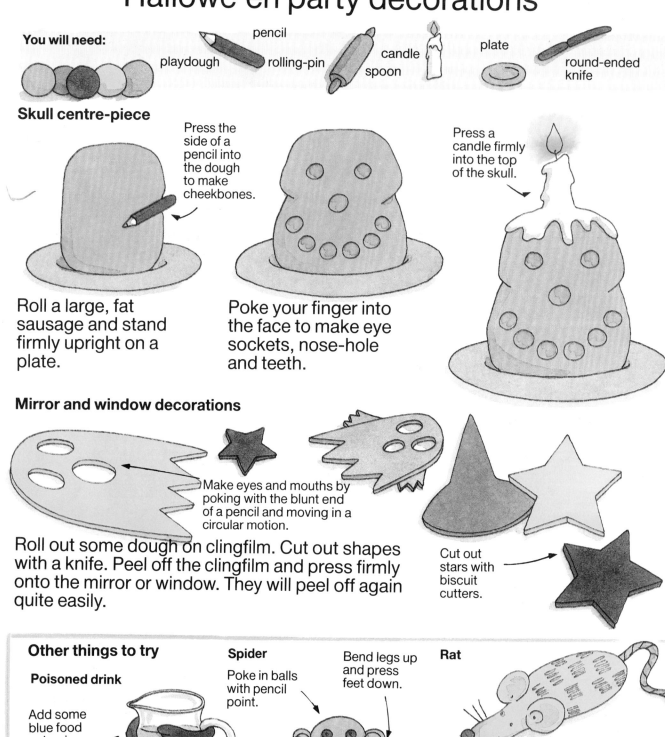

playdough pencil rolling-pin candle spoon plate round-ended knife

Skull centre-piece

Press the side of a pencil into the dough to make cheekbones.

Press a candle firmly into the top of the skull.

Roll a large, fat sausage and stand firmly upright on a plate.

Poke your finger into the face to make eye sockets, nose-hole and teeth.

Mirror and window decorations

Make eyes and mouths by poking with the blunt end of a pencil and moving in a circular motion.

Roll out some dough on clingfilm. Cut out shapes with a knife. Peel off the clingfilm and press firmly onto the mirror or window. They will peel off again quite easily.

Cut out stars with biscuit cutters.

Other things to try

Poisoned drink

Add some blue food colouring and stir.

Wind a long playdough snake around a glass jug of lemonade.

Spider

Poke in balls with pencil point.

Bend legs up and press feet down.

Mark mouth with dessert spoon.

Put a ball of dough on a small plate. Add some sausages for legs.

Rat

Add whiskers cut from a nylon brush.

Make a large version of the mouse on page 8 . Mark in its fur with a fork and add string for a tail.

serving bowl

pasta shapes

glass jug

string

clingfilm

torches

Ghostly hands

Roll two golf ball sized pieces of playdough.

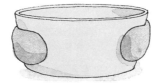

Flatten them onto the outside of a large serving bowl.

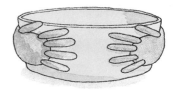

Add four sausage-shaped fingers and a shorter thumb.

Press some smaller sausages onto the ends of the fingers for nails.

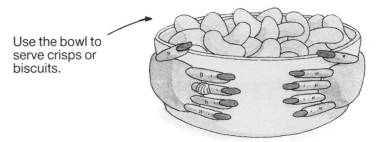

Use the bowl to serve crisps or biscuits.

Add a pasta shell "ring" and mark in the finger joints by pressing with a knife.

Spooky flashlight

Press a ball of dough over the centre of the face of a flashlight. Make a face by pressing in the flat end of a pencil and moving it in a circular motion until a hole appears; mark the eyes, nose and mouth. Shine the light in the dark for a spooky effect. Try flashing it on and off quickly.

Dinner on a plate

rolling-pin

children's scissors

round-ended knife

playdough

Menu

Sausage
Egg
Chips
Peas

Apple pie

Peas

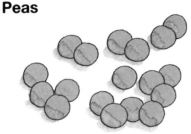

Roll small balls of green dough and press them lightly together.

Sausages

Roll fat sausages of brown dough. Prick them with a fork.

Eggs

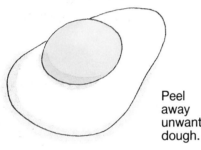

Flatten a ball of white dough. Press a smaller ball of yellow on the top for the yolk.

Chips

Lift off the chips with a fish slice.

Peel away unwanted dough.

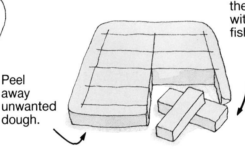

Roll some dough out thickly and cut in straight lines across and downwards.

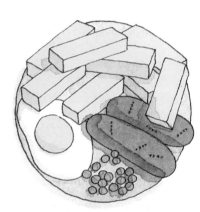

Arrange the food on a plate.

Other things to try

Hot dog
Make a bread roll with two sausage shapes of dough. Sandwich a sausage in the middle.

Fish fingers
Cut from thick, orange dough, as for chips above. To make a crumby surface, scratch with a fork.

Olive

Sweetcorn

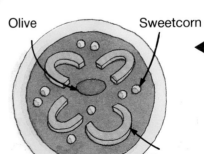

Pizza
Press out some dough to almost cover a small plate. Decorate with shapes cut from rolled dough and small rolled balls.

Peppers

fork

clingfilm

plates

fish slice

Pastry pie with roses

Press out or pat a large ball of dough onto a plate, turned upside-down, for the pie-crust.

Pinch round the edge to make a wavy pattern, or press the knife-blade gently all round the edge to decorate.

Snip some steam-holes in a pattern with some scissors.

Pastry roses

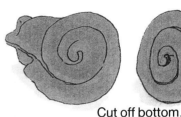

Cut off bottom.

Roll out some dough and cut into long strips, one for each rose.

Roll up the strips. Pinch the pastry together near the base of the roll.

Pull the outside pastry gently outwards to look like wavy petals.

Cut out some leaves. Mark them with a knife and arrange on top of the pie with the roses.

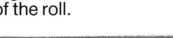

Jellies and other ideas

Press playdough into wetted moulds and gently pull it out. Use small jelly-moulds or bun trays. Roll a red cherry to decorate.

Ice cream

Press balls of dough into a dish. Roll small red balls for cherries. Cut out a wafer with a knife.

Happy birthday cake

Make a big birthday cake, decorate it and add some candles. After the candles and singing cut the cake into slices.

21

Bread and cakes

Swiss roll

Peel away unwanted dough.

Roll out dough thinly. Cut a rectangular shape.

Lift one short edge gently with a knife. Roll up the dough.

Glaze and bake. Draw in the jam with felt-tip pen.

Fruit cake

Flatten a ball of dough, then poke it with a pencil point. Bake and paint.

Jam tarts

Paint the centres red to look like jam.

Roll small balls of dough. Press the flat end of a pencil into the centre of each. Glaze, then bake them.

Chocolate eclairs

Roll out two long sausages. Press one lightly on top of the other. Bake and paint them.

Hints

Place the items on the baking tray before moulding and glazing.

Remember to remove any plastic from bottle lids before cooking.

Serve on plates made from jam-jar lids, lined with doilies or kitchen roll cut to fit.

 lightly-oiled baking tray

 metal bottle-top

 doilies or kitchen paper

 plates

 clingfilm

Cherry buns

Roll small balls of dough.

Add a tiny ball for a cherry.

Flatten small balls between your fingers for icing.

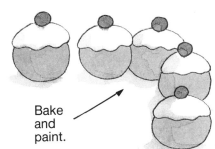

Bake and paint.

French sticks

Make cuts with knife.

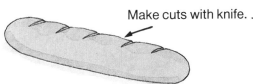

Roll a long sausage. Glaze and bake.

Granary loaf

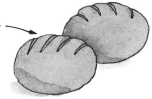

Roll a ball of dough. Glaze, bake and paint.

Cottage loaf

Roll a ball of dough. Add a smaller ball and poke in with a pencil.

Rolls and biscuits

 Mark with a pencil.

Roll small balls of dough for rolls. For biscuits flatten them between your fingers.

Pies

 Don't fill it right to the top.

Roll a ball of dough and press into a bottle lid.

Decorate it with a small ball of dough. Mark it with a straw. Bake and paint.

Scones

 Dip pen top in flour before cutting.

Squeeze to release dough.

Roll out some dough, not too thinly. Cut out some scone shapes with a pen top. Bake.

23

Baker's shop

You will need:  adult-sized shoe box with a lid | glue paint | thin card playdough | round-ended scissors | doily, kitchen roll or tissue paper | egg carton or empty yoghurt pots | used matches felt-tip pen wool

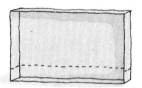

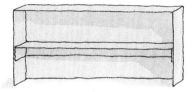

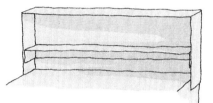

Cut a 2.5cm strip from the long side of the box lid, to make a shelf.

Cover the sides of the shelf with glue and press it firmly into the lid.

Glue the lid onto the back of the upturned box to a depth of 2.5cm.

Ideas for your shop

Bread baskets

Use individual sections of an egg carton or cut-down yoghurt pots.

Cut out a piece of card, write the shop name on it, and glue it to the top of the lid at the back.

Price tickets

Stick small pieces of card onto used matches. Press into a ball of dough.

Wrappers

Thread small squares of tissue paper or kitchen roll with wool. Make a hole with a pencil point in the side of the counter. Poke a used match in to make a hook. Hang the wrappers up.

Try making a butcher's shop with hams, chops and sausages, or a fish stall with lots of different fish.

Allow the glue to dry, then paint the shop. Line the shelf with kitchen roll or doilies, glued in position. Arrange your bread and cakes.

Picnic food

You will need: saltdough* round-ended knife drinking straw paints egg glaze (see page 29) felt-tip pens pastry cutters or aerosol can lids kitchen roll round-ended scissors

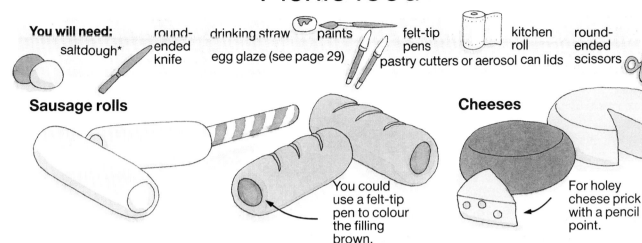

Sausage rolls

You could use a felt-tip pen to colour the filling brown.

Roll small sausages then press a straw into each end to make the filling.

Make cuts across the top with a knife. Glaze them, then bake them.

Cheeses

For holey cheese prick with a pencil point.

Flatten a ball into a disc. Cut wedges. Bake, cool, then paint.

Sandwiches

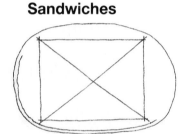

Roll out dough about 1cm thick. Cut a square with a knife, then cut into quarters.

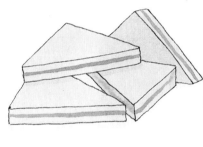

Separate the four pieces and bake. Draw a felt-tip line round each piece for the filling.

Ideas for your picnic

Hamper
Use a hinged egg carton. Make holes for wool or ribbon handles by pushing a pencil point through the cardboard.

Beakers
Use toothpaste tube caps or bottle tops.

Tablecloth
Use a square of kitchen paper decorated with dots of felt-tip.

Plates
Make them from dough, or use jar lids.

Bring some food along from the baker's shop and the vegetable stall.

Napkins
Cut small squares of kitchen paper and fold into four. You can make napkin rings by fastening long sausage shapes into a circle, baking and painting.

*To find out about making and baking saltdough, see page 30.

Fruit and vegetable stall

You will need: saltdough* round-ended knife pencil lightly-oiled baking tray sellotape cooling tray egg boxes paint oven gloves felt-tip pens card and glue

Potatoes

Roll small balls. Squash into knobbly shapes. Mark eyes with pencil point.

Peppers

Roll short, fat sausages. Make criss cross marks with a knife across the top.

Cucumbers

Roll long sausages, thinner at one end than the other. Make long marks lengthways with a knife.

Marrows

Roll fat sausages. Draw in stripes with felt-tip pens.

Cauliflower
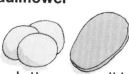
Push three small balls of white dough together. Flatten small green balls of dough to make leaves. Overlap the leaves round the centre. Mark the centre with a pencil point.

Carrots

Roll sausage shapes thinner at one end. Add some green leaves and make marks around the carrots with a knife.

Apples

Roll small balls and poke a pencil point into the tops.

Bananas

Roll sausage shapes and curve them. Draw on felt-tip markings.

Oranges

Roll small balls. Mark peel with pencil point.

Spring onions
Roll very skinny sausages and press them together into bundles. Colour the ends green.

*To find out about making, baking and colouring saltdough, see page 30.

Glue on a sign for the stall. → my stall

Put all your fruit and vegetables into an egg box.

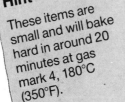

Hint
These items are small and will bake hard in around 20 minutes at gas mark 4, 180°C (350°F).

Use cut-down sections of egg box for additional baskets.

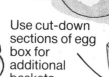

26

Using playdough as a mould

You will need: 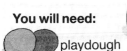 plaster-of-paris 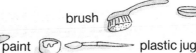 brush jar lids round-ended knife
 playdough rolling-pin paint plastic jug water

Badge

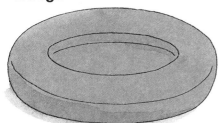

Roll out a disc of playdough at least 3cms thick. Press the jar lid firmly into the dough to make a round well.

Collect some small objects, such as the ones above, from around the house. You could also use small plastic toys.

Press the objects into the playdough inside the well. Don't press them too deep. Lift them out carefully.

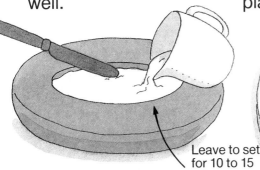

Leave to set for 10 to 15 minutes.

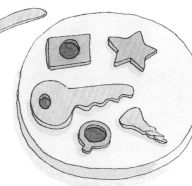

Mix up the plaster and pour it into the well. Gently slap the surface with a knife to get rid of air bubbles.

When dry, carefully pull off the playdough. Scrub the plaster clean with a washing up brush, under a tap.

Allow to dry thoroughly, then paint. Fix a safety-pin on the back with sticking plaster (see page 7).

Other things to try
Name plaque
Roll out some dough quite thickly and press a date-box lid upside down into it to make a frame.

Write your name on greaseproof paper and turn it over to use as a pattern.

Press plastic letters into the dough, following the pattern. Pour in plaster. Allow it to set. Scrub and paint.

Hand moulds
Press your foot or outspread hand into a thick piece of rolled-out dough. Lift it out carefully to leave a clear outline. Pour in plaster and leave it to set.

Allow to dry thoroughly, then paint.

Hint

Don't dispose of wet plaster down the sink. Put it in a plastic bag, allow it to set, then put it in the rubbish bin.

Dough shapes you can eat

You will need:

1 packet/ 283gms/ 10oz of plain white bread-mix

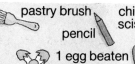

pastry brush

pencil

child's scissors

1 egg beaten with 1 tbsp of water

round-ended knife

oiled baking-tray

teaspoon

fish slice

cooling rack

oven gloves

clingfilm

flour

When you have made the shapes you want, leave them to rise in a warm place for between 30 and 55 mins. Glaze them then bake as specified on packet.

Butterfly

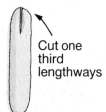

Cut one third lengthways

Roll a long sausage. Snip one end with some scissors

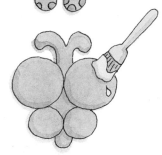

Make wings by flattening balls. Press them onto the body.

Curl the snipped dough round to make antennae.

Tortoise

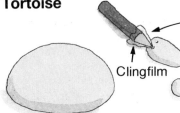

Mark in the eyes with a pencil point.

Clingfilm

Pat a piece of dough into a dome shape.

Roll out shapes for a head, legs and tail.

Mark the shell with a knife.

Lift up the edges and tuck the feet, head and tail underneath.

Hints

Where pieces of dough need joining, dip a finger in water and wet both surfaces.

Work directly onto the baking tray to avoid spoiling shapes when you move them.

Always handle the dough on a lightly-floured surface.

Other ideas

Try the snake on page 9, or the hedgehog on page 10.

Letter buns

Using sausage shapes of dough make the letters of your name.

Octopus

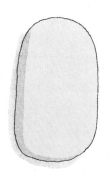

Press on eyes with pencil point.

Mark mouth with teaspoon.

Roll a fat sausage and press it out into an oblong.

Make tentacles by snipping with scissors.

Pull down tentacles and curl around.

Playdough and saltdough

You can buy playdough in toyshops or large newsagents or you can make it yourself. You simply mix the ingredients and heat them on a stove, or in a microwave oven.

If you want to make things that will go hard so you can keep them and play with them, you need to use saltdough.

To make saltdough you combine the ingredients without cooking them. When you have made what you want you can harden it by baking it in the oven.

The things you will need for each project in the book are listed across the top of each page. Sometimes playdough is specified, sometimes saltdough with baking and painting instructions. However, if you want to you can do all the projects with playdough or with saltdough.

How to make playdough

Ingredients:

200g plain flour

100g salt

2 tsps cream of tartar

1tbs oil

300ml water

A few drops of food colouring

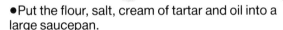

- Put the flour, salt, cream of tartar and oil into a large saucepan.
- Add the food colouring to the water.
- Add the liquid gradually to the ingredients in the saucepan and mix it in thoroughly to get rid of as many lumps as possible.
- Put the pan over a medium-low heat and cook, stirring constantly. This is quite hard work. The mixture will be very liquid at first, then begin to thicken suddenly.
- Continue to stir until the dough becomes very stiff.
- Remove the pan from the heat and scrape out the dough with a wooden spoon onto a smooth surface.
- Put the pan to soak immediately.

Warning: playdough looks very tempting at this stage, but the inside will still be very hot, even when the outside has cooled. Before using, slice it in half with a knife and test it warily with your finger.

- Knead it thoroughly until it becomes smooth and pliable and holds its shape well.

Using a microwave

This method involves much less physical effort and produces excellent results. The instructions given are for a 650 watt oven. Adjust accordingly.

- Mix the ingredients as for pan-cooked playdough (see below left) but use a large bowl suitable for microwave use.
- Put the bowl, uncovered in the microwave.
- Cook at full power for one minute.
- Using oven gloves remove it from the oven and stir well.
- Replace the bowl and continue cooking until the mixture starts to leave the side of the bowl and becomes very stiff – approximately 2-2½ minutes. (Stir at least once during this time.)
- Using oven gloves, remove from the oven onto a heatproof surface.
- Scrape out the dough with a wooden spoon onto a smooth surface.
- Knead as before.

Storing playdough

Playdough needs to be kept in an airtight container to stop it drying out.

Bought playdough should keep indefinitely when stored in its pot with the lid firmly on.

Store homemade playdough in a polythene food bag, inside an airtight box or jar.

If left exposed to the air a salty crust will form on it. You can rescue it by kneading it thoroughly with a little oil.

Colour mixing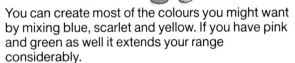

You can create most of the colours you might want by mixing blue, scarlet and yellow. If you have pink and green as well it extends your range considerably.

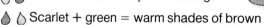

- Blue + scarlet = brown
- Blue + pink = purple/mauve
- Blue + yellow = green
- Yellow + scarlet or pink = orange
- Scarlet + green = warm shades of brown
- Green + yellow = acid green
- Green + blue = dark leaf green

Experiment with different combinations. Mix colours on saucers first, before adding them to the water.

Build up a library of colours. Make smaller quantities of those you think you will use least.

The colour will not come out onto your hands during use, but it is advisable to keep it off carpets.

Saltdough

Saltdough recipe

Ingredients:

300g plain flour

300g salt

1 tbs oil

Approximately 200ml water

- Mix all the ingredients in a large bowl using a knife. The dough should feel pliable – add more liquid if necessary.
- Turn out onto a floured surface and knead thoroughly until very smooth and elastic.

Saltdough improves with keeping. Its texture becomes finer and less grainy. It is best made the day before you need it.

Warning
Salt can sting. Protect small cuts and grazes on the hand with sticking-plaster.

Storing saltdough

The uncooked dough keeps indefinitely in a plastic bag in the fridge. If it goes a little soft, knead some flour into it before use.

Colouring saltdough

You can colour saltdough while you are making it by adding food colouring to the mixing water. The colour will go a little lighter when the dough is baked.

Where small quantities of coloured dough are needed, as for the vegetables on page 26, mix the colours you want on separate saucers, then knead in small portions of white uncooked dough until evenly coloured.

Painting

Instead of using food colouring you can paint saltdough after it has been baked. Use powder, poster or watercolour paints.

You could just add the finishing touches with paint or felt-tip pens.

Painting will soften the dough temporarily. Allow it to dry out again in the air or still warm oven. Place painted items on a cake cooling rack to dry quickly without spoiling.

Glazing

This gives dough a lovely golden brown colour. Try it for the miniature breads on page 23.

Simply beat a whole egg and paint onto the uncooked saltdough with a pastry brush or paintbrush.

Baking saltdough

Cook small items for between 10 and 20 minutes, depending on their size, on a lightly-oiled baking tray or roasting tin at gas mark 4, 350F, 180C in the centre of the oven.

Larger items are best cooked overnight at gas mark ½, 250F, 130C. This avoids the dangers of cracking or the dough beginning to brown on the outside while the centre is still uncooked. Precoloured dough may brown very slightly on cooking. The dough is also liable to balloon out of shape if cooked at too high a temperature.

Don't worry if the inside is still a little spongy even after cooking overnight; the salt in the dough acts as a preservative and the centre will air-dry and harden after a while. The larger and thicker the item the longer the drying-out time will be.

You can safely bake small items with larger ones overnight at a low temperature.

Do not use thin trays or cake tins if cooking overnight; they will brown and spoil and scorch coloured dough.

There may be some cracking if your oven is too hot. This is usually underneath the piece and does not spoil the look of the finished article. Experience will tell you how the dough behaves in your own oven.

Saltdough expands slightly on cooking. Keep this in mind while shaping. Make good-sized holes for threading, so they don't close up during baking.

Microwave ovens are not suitable for baking saltdough. The dough tends to balloon out of shape and the salt burns easily.

Always warn of the dangers of a hot oven or baking tray and make a noticeable display of wearing oven gloves.

Tools

Surfaces to work on

Work on smooth surfaces such as formica or polyurethaned wood, or turn trays upside down so that the rim does not get in the way. You can also work on large flat books wrapped in clingfilm.

Playdough rolled out onto a piece of clingfilm lifts and peels off beautifully, leaving a lovely smooth surface on the underside.

When working with saltdough lightly dust the surface with flour.

Tools you may need

 A rolling-pin. You could use a piece of dowelling, or a broom handle instead, or use one from a child's baking set.

 Knives. For safety always use round-ended ones. Plastic knives are safe and light to handle.

 Scissors. For safety use round-ended ones and child-sized ones for easy use. Use for snipping raised patterns (e.g. the hedgehog's quills on page 10), or cutting dough cleanly to mark in mouths and so on.

 Forks. Use for scratching or pressing patterns into the dough, or for scratching two surfaces to be joined. Plastic forks are light and easy to handle, but be careful the prongs are still sharp.

 Spoons. These are very useful for marking curved mouth shapes. Use the side of a dessert-spoon for a large mouth and the tip of a teaspoon for a small one.

 Sieve. A large-meshed metal one is best. These can be used to push dough through so it forms fine strings. Push clumps gently together to make bushes (page 5), or hair for figures or animals. It may help to wet the sieve, shaking off excess water, to enable the dough to be pushed through more easily.

Use the sieve also for washing small objects, like buttons or beads, which are smeary after being pushed into dough. Put them in the sieve, then swish them around in warm soapy water. Rinse them under the tap, then turn them out onto a kitchen roll to dry.

 Pencil. This is very useful for pressing in eyes with the pointed end, making patterns with either end, or pressed sideways into the dough. Alternatively use a child's knitting needle.

 Cutters. Use scone or biscuit cutters, upturned plastic tumblers, or plastic tops from aerosol cans (flour lightly before use, squeeze gently to release dough). Plastic pen tops make tiny cutters (e.g. for miniature scones on page 23).

 Fish slice. This is useful for lifting and transferring pieces without damage, or removing hot saltdough items from baking tray to cooling rack, or pressing patterns into dough.

 Other tools. Straws, used matchsticks, keys, pasta, beads, buttons, shells, pebbles. Anything which will make a clear imprint in dough can be used to build up a pattern.

 Moulds. Small bun trays or jelly moulds can be used. Push dough firmly into the wetted mould. Ease away from the sides and pull out gently to make "cakes" and "jellies". Try using the moulded plastic containers from chocolate or toy-packaging.

 Use playdough itself as a mould. Impressions can be made in the dough and a cast taken with plaster (see page 27).

Techniques

Starting off
Once they have learnt how to make some simple, basic shapes children will soon be able to decide how to go about putting their own ideas into practice. The projects in this book are mostly created from varying sizes of ball shapes or sausage shapes.

Rolling balls

Show children how to pinch off a piece of dough and press it into a rough ball shape.
- Place it on the flat palm of an open hand.
- Lay the other hand on top and roll gently between the palms with a circular motion.
- Turn the ball a few times in between rolling until you have a good shape.
- Or place the roughly-shaped ball onto a smooth surface and roll with a circular movement under your open palm.
- To roll several balls of the same size pinch off a piece of dough, divide it into two, then divide each piece in two, and so on until you have the number you want. This way you can make ears, feet and so on that match in size.
- Tiny balls for noses, buttons and so on can be rolled in the palm of your hand with a finger-end. The ball will stick to the end of your finger; lift gently and press in position.

Discs
- These can be made by patting a ball evenly with the palm of your hand, or flattening a ball directly onto the model with a finger. You can also roll out the dough and cut a shape, using a suitably sized cutter.

Rolling sausage-shapes

- Break off a piece of dough, then roll it into a ball shape. Either roll the ball gently between the palms of your hands, or place on a smooth surface and roll lightly back and forward.
- Long sausage-shapes can be rolled using two hands at once, with closed fingers. Move from the centre outwards as you roll, to lengthen the dough.
- Or roll with the palm of the hand on first one section, then another, to keep thicknesses even.
- Rolling to a pointed end (for tails etc.) Roll out a sausage shape, then continue to roll at one end only with most pressure on the outside of your palm, until a point is formed. A really fine point can be made by continuing to roll with a finger end.

Rolling out dough
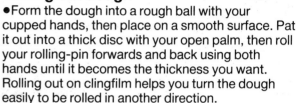
- Form the dough into a rough ball with your cupped hands, then place on a smooth surface. Pat it out into a thick disc with your open palm, then roll your rolling-pin forwards and back using both hands until it becomes the thickness you want. Rolling out on clingfilm helps you turn the dough easily to be rolled in another direction.
- To roll long thin shapes make a sausage shape and roll out as above.

Using cutters
- These should be plastic, not metal. A metal cutter accidentally placed the wrong way up and pressed hard, could result in a cut hand.
- Press the cutter gently into the dough with the flat of your hand, then more firmly once it has bitten. Wriggle it slightly from side to side to make sure it has cut right through.
- Lift off the unwanted dough from round the cut shape. This leaves it free to be lifted elsewhere on a fish slice, or decorated.

Free-hand cutting
This is best done with a round-ended knife, preferably plastic.
- Roll the dough out evenly and draw the shape you want onto it with the knife, before cutting.
- You can use a paper pattern as a guide. Lay it on the dough and cut round it.
- Use a ruler to help you cut straight lines.
- Don't try to turn a corner in the dough with the knife. Make each cut longer than you need, criss-crossing at the corners each time to leave the shape you require (see page 2, caterpillar on a leaf).

Joining pieces of dough
- To make pieces of dough stick together it helps if you scratch both surfaces with your knife and moisten the dough a little with a wet finger.
- You can use a piece cut from a drinking straw to help you join pieces.
- Another way of joining two pieces of dough is to shape one into a point and make a hole in the other piece for a point to fit into.

Decorating dough
This can be done in a variety of ways: poking with fingers, pinching, pressing with various parts of the hand, making imprints with a variety of objects (see tools) or decorating with buttons, beads or pasta. Experiment with anything which makes a sharp outline or interesting shape.

PAPERPLAY

There is a great variety of things you can make using paper or card, scissors and glue, with a few extras. This book is designed to give you some ideas and starting points. Besides being fun, this type of activity can help young children to develop important skills such as hand control and coordination, concentration and decision-making, and broaden their understanding of concepts such as size, shape and measurement.

Bee mobile

You will need: two colours of paper · pencil · ruler · round-ended scissors · paper glue · wool · white paper · felt-tip pen

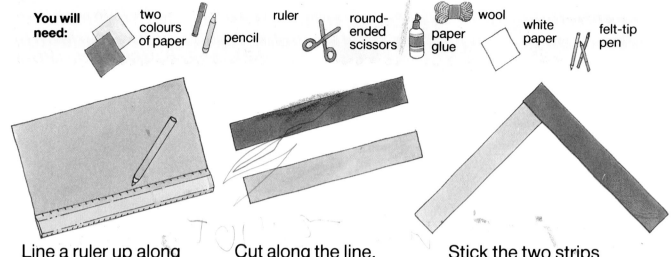

Line a ruler up along the edge of a piece of coloured paper. Draw a line.

Cut along the line. Make another strip using different coloured paper.

Stick the two strips together at one end, at right angles.

Repeat until all the paper is used up.

Stick the last piece down firmly.

Fold paper to cut two the same size.

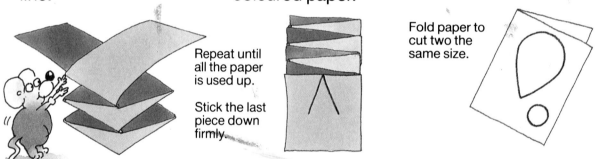

Bend the bottom strip up and over the top strip. Press firmly.

Cut an upside down V shape into an end piece. Bend it down to make a nose.

Cut two wings and two eyes out of paper.

Tie on a thread.

Stick on the wings.

Draw in eyes and stick them on.

Pull body into concertina shape.

Draw in mouth.

To make mobiles

Tie sticks of different ▶ lengths together. Plant support sticks are ideal.

Make several bees and hang them on threads from a coathanger. ▼

34

Snail mobile

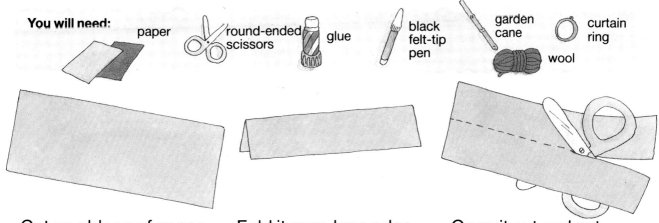

You will need: paper — round-ended scissors — glue — black felt-tip pen — garden cane — wool — curtain ring

Cut an oblong of paper about 16cm by 3cm.

Fold it over, long edge to long edge. Press to make a crease.

Open it out and cut along the crease to make two strips.

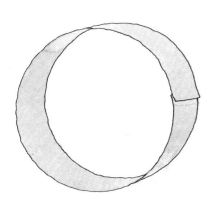

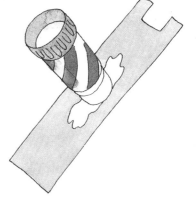

Put glue on one end of one strip. Stick the other end to it to make a circle.

Cut a small square out of the other strip to leave horns. Draw on eyes and a mouth.

Turn it over and put glue on the middle section.

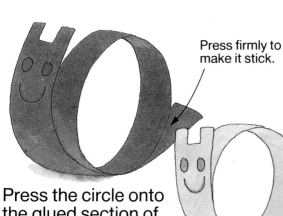

Press firmly to make it stick.

Press the circle onto the glued section of the second strip. Lift up the head end.

Making a mobile

Make several snails and use wool to hang them from a stick as shown.

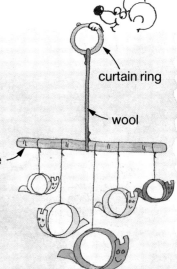

curtain ring

wool

garden cane

Balance the stick by sliding it left or right through the centre loop.

Funny faces

You will need: paper plates magazines 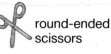 round-ended scissors glue paper or wool

Cut out lots of eyes, noses, mouths and eyebrows from magazines.

Move them around a paper plate until you have the face you want, then stick them down. Add wool or paper hair if you like.

More simple collage ideas

Fridge food

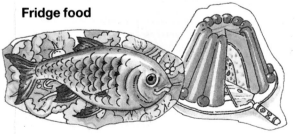

Discuss what kind of food you keep in the fridge and why. Stick some pictures of the food onto strong paper and cut round them. Fix onto the fridge to decorate it.

Car park
Draw out a car park. Discuss how you will arrange and stick down pictures of cars and lorries so they won't block each other in.

Tea table
Stick down paper doilies, or napkins for a tablecloth. Add pictures of cakes, cutlery, cups and plates.

Bendy snakes

You will need: magazines   glue   paper   scissors   felt-tip pens   ruler

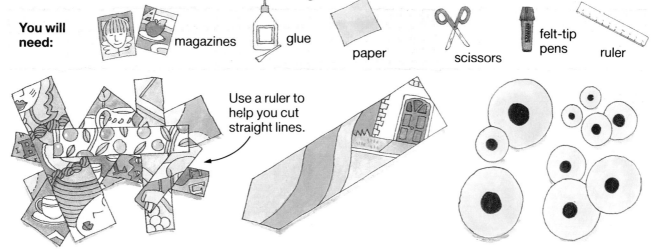

Use a ruler to help you cut straight lines.

Cut lots of coloured strips, some wide, some narrow, some long, some short, from a magazine.

Cut one end into a pointed tail, the other into a rounded head.

Draw and cut out lots of eyes. To get two eyes the same size, cut through two layers of paper.

Stick the eyes onto the heads of the snakes.

Turn the snakes over and put blobs of glue down their backs.

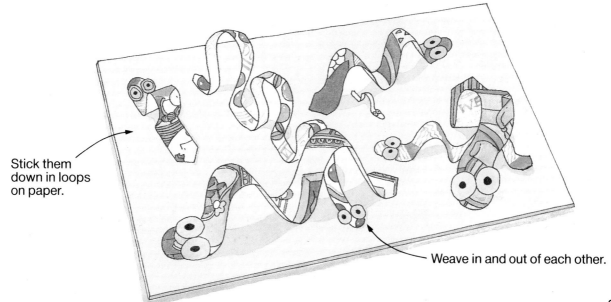

Stick them down in loops on paper.

Weave in and out of each other.

37

Trapeze artiste

You will need: wire coathanger, straw, pointed scissors, round-ended scissors, greaseproof paper, sticky tape, decorations (see opposite page), felt-tips, paper-clips

To make the trapeze

Bend a wire coathanger to make a corner about 8cm from the hook.

Do the same on the other side.

Make some straight sides.

Straighten out the bottom bar.

Cut a piece of straw the same length as the bottom bar. Make a slit along it with pointed scissors*.

Press the straw onto the bottom bar. It should spin freely.

Lay some greaseproof paper on the template opposite. Secure it with paper-clips. Trace the figure with a thick crayon.

Colour the figure and draw in the face. Cut neatly round the outline, then stick on some decorations (see opposite).

Attach your person to the bar by curling her hands over and taping them in position.

Make her somersault over the bar, or hang the trapeze in a doorway, suspended from a piece of wool. Push it to make her fly through the air. Try putting her limbs in different positions.

38

*An adult should make the slit.

Some ideas for decorating the costume

◀ Felt-tip pens

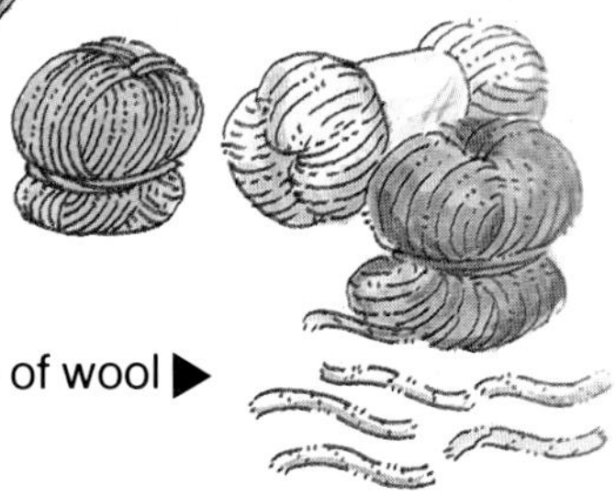

Scraps of wool ▶

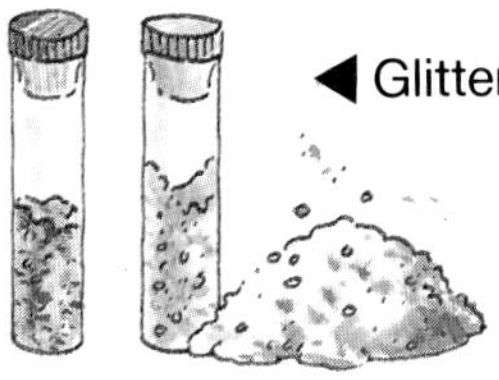

◀ Glitter

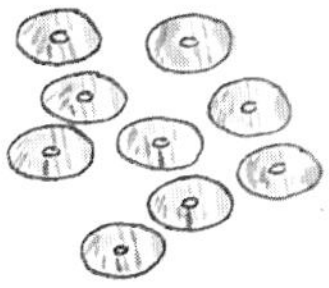

Sequins ▶

Feathers from a feather duster. ▼

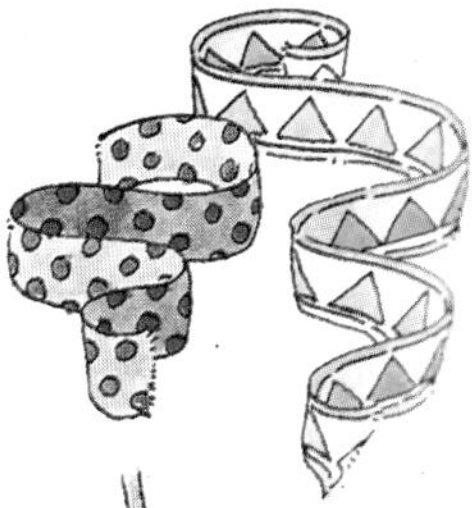

Gummed paper shapes ▲

Ribbon ▶

Other ways to decorate your trapeze artiste

Give her wool hair. Only use a little, or the head will be too heavy.

Tie bows round her legs and arms. Use wool or silk thread.

Trace round the line and cut out.

Owl and pussycat

You will need:
 wallpaper
 gluestick
 round-ended scissors
 saucer

To make the pussycat

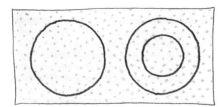

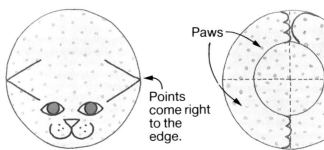

Paws

Tail

Points come right to the edge.

Make two circles on a piece of wallpaper by drawing round a saucer. Cut them out. Inside one, use a jar lid to draw a smaller circle.

Cut two V shapes for the ears in the plain circle. Draw a cat's face on the front half.

Fold the second circle into quarters, then open it out. Draw and cut out two paws and a tail.

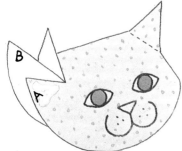

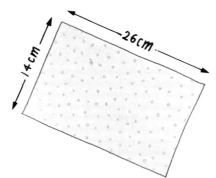

26cm

14cm

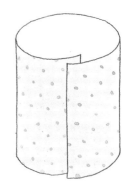

Complete the head by bending up the ears. Glue the underside of point B and overlap onto point A each side.

Using more wallpaper, draw and cut out a rectangle, 14cm by 26cm.

Bend the rectangle into a cylinder, overlapping it by about 2cm. Stick the ends together.

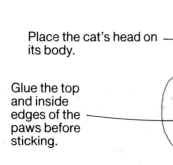

Place the cat's head on its body.

Glue the top and inside edges of the paws before sticking.

Stick the tail on so that it can be seen from the front.

Hint

To make a nice even cylinder shape, wrap the paper strip round a can of food. Stick down the edges, then slide the tin out.

 jam-jar lids
 felt-tip pens
 ruler
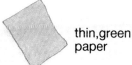 thin, green paper

To make the owl

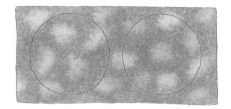

Make two circles on a piece of wallpaper by drawing round a saucer. Cut them out.

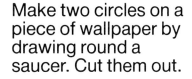

On one circle draw and cut out ears. Give your owl large round eyes and a beak.

Fold the other circle in half. Snip with scissors around the lower quarters, then cut down the fold line.

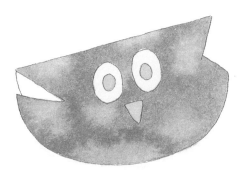

Complete the head as for the cat, but do not bend the ears up.

Cut a rectangle as for the cat. Bend the strip into a cylinder and stick down.

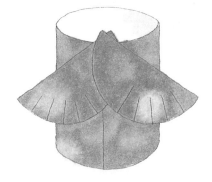

Overlap the wings and stick them together. Stick the wings to the cylinder.

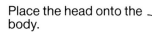
Place the head onto the body.

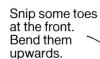
Snip some toes at the front. Bend them upwards.

Other ideas to try

Make an owl or a cat family. Use jar lids for templates to make kittens and owlets. Make the bodies smaller too.

To make a tree for your owl make a bigger version of the sea anemone on page 43.

41

Magic boxes

You will need:

shoe box with lid

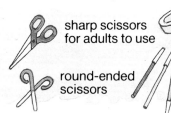
sharp scissors for adults to use

sticky tape

round-ended scissors

felt-tip pens

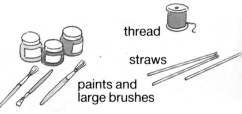
thread

straws

paints and large brushes

Flying ghost box

Use a ruler to help you draw the borders.

Turn a shoe box onto one long side. Cut out the top, using sharp scissors*, leaving a 2cm border on three sides.

Pierce a hole in the lid with sharp scissors*. Cut out the centre, leaving a 2cm border all the way round.

Cut a hole in one side, so you can shine a torch into the box with the light off.

Stick lid on to front of box.

Paint the inside of the box.

Stick on torn strips of paper for trunks and branches.

To make a ghost, pinch a piece of white toilet tissue in the centre, so that the corners hang down. Draw on black eyes. Hang from a thread fastened to a straw.

Add a bat to swoop around.

Draw some strange shapes for spooks. Colour them and cut them out. Hang them from straws.

Cut a trap door out of paper. Stick one side to the floor, so that it can move up and down.

Glue the bottom onto the floor of the box. Pull the thread to make it jump up.

Jumping-up skeleton

Draw a skeleton on white paper and then cut an outline round it.

Fold it as shown and attach a thread to the back of its head with sticky tape.

*An adult should do the cutting.

42

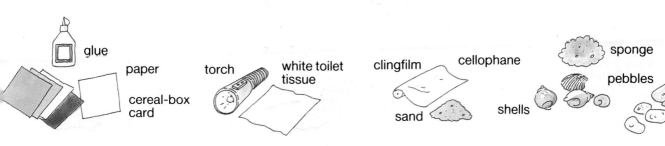

glue

paper

cereal-box card

torch

white toilet tissue

clingfilm

cellophane

sand

shells

sponge

pebbles

Aquarium

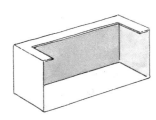

Cut out the side of the box and the lid as for the ghost box.

Paint blue water and a yellow, sandy floor inside the box.

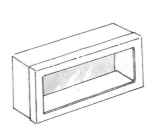

Use tape to stick clingfilm over the inside of the lid, so that it looks like glass.

Glue or tape the lid onto the front.

Stick torn coloured strips onto the sides to make seaweed or coral.

Draw fish on card or paper. Colour both sides and cut out. Attach thread and hang from straws.

Put shells, pebbles, bits of sponge and sand on the bottom. If you have no sand you can colour a little sugar with drops of food colouring.

Cut out and hang a cellophane jellyfish.

To make a sea-snake, see the bendy snakes on page 37.

To make an octopus, copy the spider on page 50.

Sea anemone

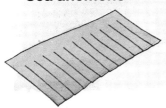

Cut slits in a strip of paper.

Roll the paper up and tape it at the bottom.

Gently pull the centre up.

Stand it upright by pressing it into a ball of dough or plasticine.

43

Super-glider

You will need:

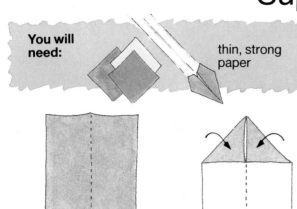

thin, strong paper

ruler

round-ended scissors

pencil

glue

large-headed drawing pin

straw

Measure and cut a rectangle 10cm by 15cm. Make a crease down the centre by folding it in half. Open it out and turn it over.

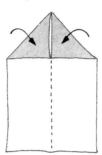

Turn the top corners down, so that the points meet in the centre.

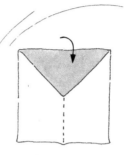

Turn the top triangle down.

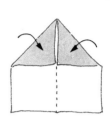

Turn the top corners down, so the points meet in the centre.

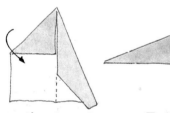

Turn the two top sides of the triangle in, so the points meet in the centre.

Fold in half, along the original centre crease.

Turn upside down. Pull the wings up until they are level. Hold between your finger and thumb underneath and launch.

Windmill

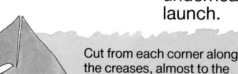

Cut a square of paper, 10cm by 10cm.

Fold diagonally to make creases.

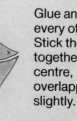

Cut from each corner along the creases, almost to the centre.

Glue and turn up every other point. Stick them together in the centre, overlapping slightly.

Press a large-headed pin through the centre of the windmill and into the top of a straw. Blow hard to make it whirl, or hold it in a strong wind.

44

Submarine

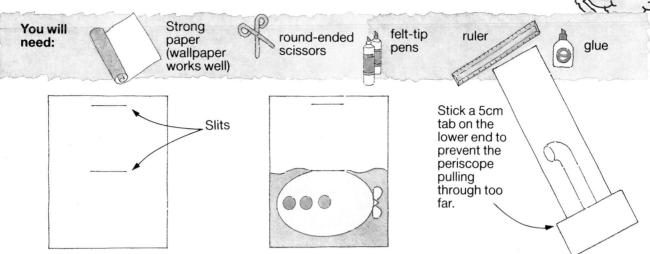

You will need: Strong paper (wallpaper works well), round-ended scissors, felt-tip pens, ruler, glue

Slits

Stick a 5cm tab on the lower end to prevent the periscope pulling through too far.

Cut a sheet of paper about 12cm by 15cm. Make two 4cm slits, one half-way down, one near the top.

Draw the surface of the sea and a submarine, making its top level with the lower slit. Colour them in.

Cut a strip 3cm wide and 4cm longer than your paper. Draw a periscope on the lower half.

Pull up or push down from the top.

Thread the strip through the slits. Pull up from the top to raise the periscope.

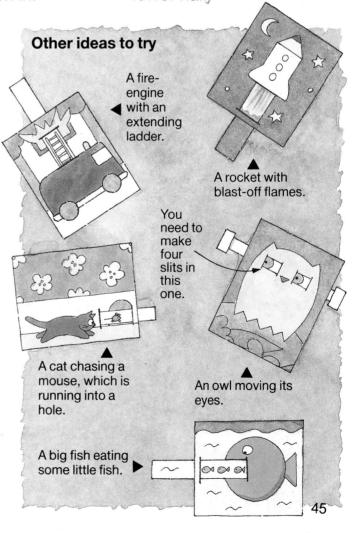

Other ideas to try

A fire-engine with an extending ladder.

A rocket with blast-off flames.

You need to make four slits in this one.

A cat chasing a mouse, which is running into a hole.

An owl moving its eyes.

A big fish eating some little fish. ▶

45

Cars and roads

You will need: stiff paper   round-ended scissors   felt-tip pens or paints

Draw cars, lorries, motorbikes, bicycles, trees, shops etc. along the straight edges of your paper. Colour them in bright colours.

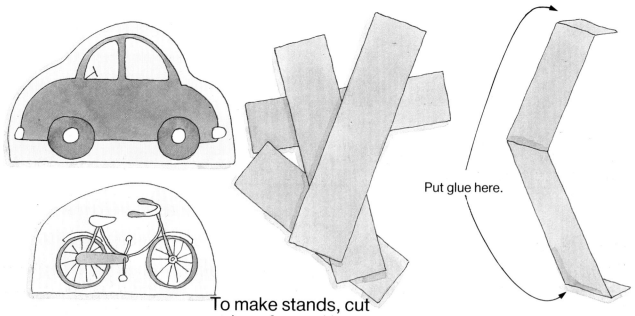

Put glue here.

Cut them out, keeping a straight edge at the bottom.

To make stands, cut strips of cereal box card about 2cm wide and twice the height of the drawing.

Fold, as shown, and put glue on the end tabs.

46

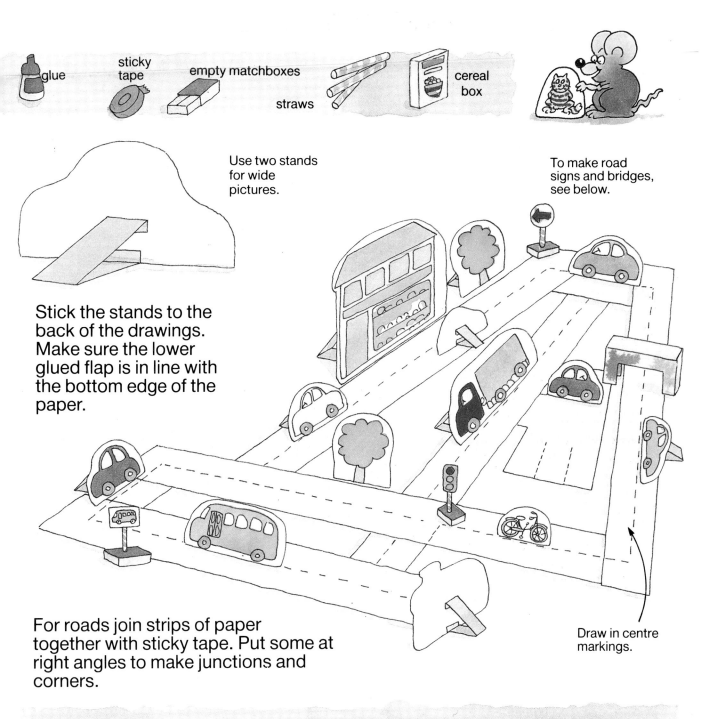

glue

sticky tape

empty matchboxes

straws

cereal box

Use two stands for wide pictures.

To make road signs and bridges, see below.

Stick the stands to the back of the drawings. Make sure the lower glued flap is in line with the bottom edge of the paper.

For roads join strips of paper together with sticky tape. Put some at right angles to make junctions and corners.

Draw in centre markings.

Other ideas to try

Road signs

Draw and cut out road signs.

Stick a cut-down straw to the back.

Make a hole in a matchbox with a pencil point. Push the straw into the hole.

Bridge

Cut a cereal box in half. Cut a rectangle wider than the road from each side.

Animal zoo

Draw and cut out lots of different animals and fix them onto stands, as for the cars and buildings above.

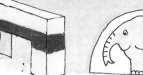

47

Paper money and wallet

You will need: white paper, coloured paper, felt-tip pens or crayons, sticky tape, glue, soft pencil, coins, ruler

Cut out some pieces of paper the size and shape of money notes. On each one write a number to show how much it is worth and draw a picture.

For your wallet, cut a piece of coloured paper 2cm wider than your paper money and one and a half times as high.

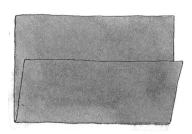

Fold up the bottom edge by about a third.

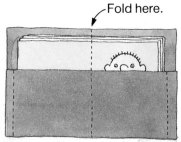

Fold here.

Stick down the sides to make a pocket. Put the money in it and fold it in half.

Write your name on the front and then decorate it.

Other ideas to try

Coins
Lay thin paper over real coins. Hold it firmly in place while you rub over them with a soft pencil. Stick card on the back and cut them out.

Stamps
Draw a small box. Draw or stick a small picture in the centre. Cut it out.

Envelopes
Fold a square of paper diagonally in both directions. Open it out.

Centre

Fold the bottom corner up to the centre. Fold in each of the two side corners, overlapping the edges slightly.

Glue or tape down the edges. Fold the remaining top corner down to make the flap.

Racing rafts

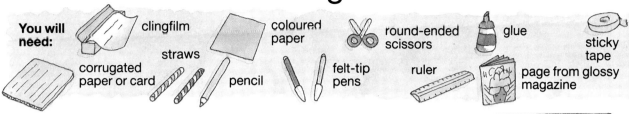

You will need: clingfilm, corrugated paper or card, straws, coloured paper, pencil, felt-tip pens, round-ended scissors, ruler, glue, page from glossy magazine, sticky tape

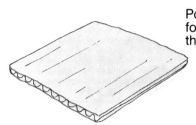

Cut a square of corrugated paper.

Poke a hole for a straw in the centre.

To make it last longer, wrap clingfilm around it and stick the edges down.

Cut out a square of coloured paper for a sail and decorate it. Poke a small hole in the centre top and bottom.

Try racing two or more rafts in the sink or bath. Blow hard into the sails.

Thread the sail onto a straw and push one end of the straw firmly into the raft. Cut the straw down if necessary.

Rowing boat

Cut a rectangle 9cm by 5cm out of glossy magazine paper. Mark the centre of each side.

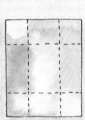

Fold each side in turn to the centre. Crease and open out.

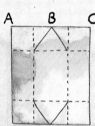

A   B   C

Make a cut from the centre of each short side to where the fold-lines cross.

A B C

◀ Bring points A and C together behind B. Glue them together where they overlap. Glue triangle B over them. Repeat at the other end.

Cut a strip of paper 7cm by 2cm. Fold down the ends 1cm. Glue and stick into the boat to make a seat.

Cut some straws and poke through the side for oars.

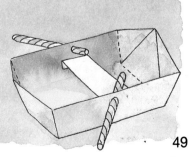

49

Paper puppets

You will need: coloured crêpe paper · paper to crumple · round-ended scissors · sticky tape · felt-tip pens · wool or elastic · glue · straws · paper

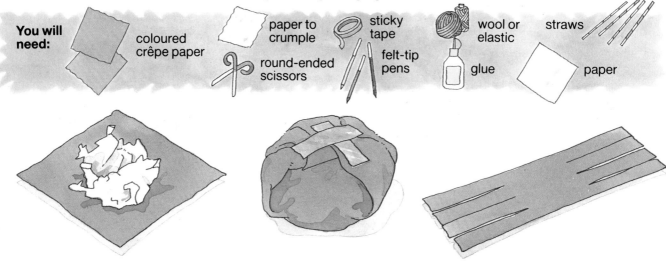

Place a crumpled ball of paper on a large square of crêpe paper.

Gather up the crêpe paper and stick it down with tape to make a ball.

Cut an oblong of coloured paper. Snip long cuts down each short side.

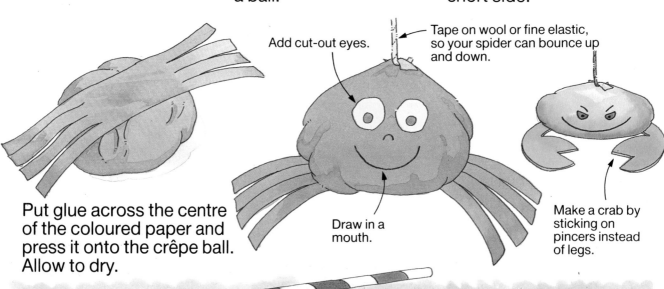

Put glue across the centre of the coloured paper and press it onto the crêpe ball. Allow to dry.

Add cut-out eyes.

Tape on wool or fine elastic, so your spider can bounce up and down.

Draw in a mouth.

Make a crab by sticking on pincers instead of legs.

Straw puppets

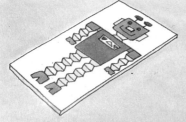

Draw and cut out some characters from a story you like.

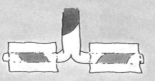

For each character cut a slit in one end of a straw.

Press the split ends onto the back of the puppet and stick down firmly to make a handle.

You will need:

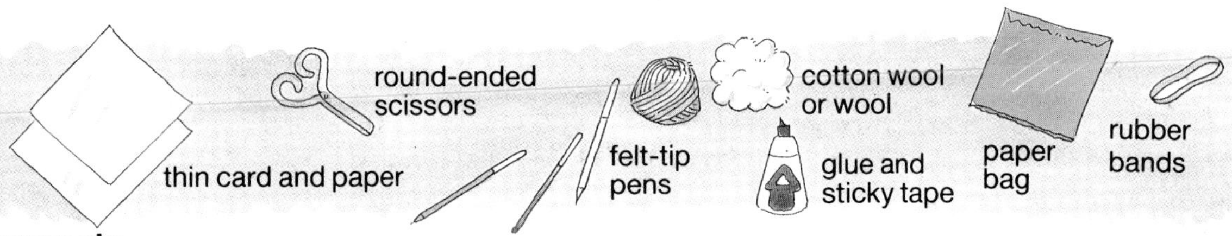

round-ended scissors

thin card and paper

felt-tip pens

cotton wool or wool

glue and sticky tape

paper bag

rubber bands

Dancing puppets

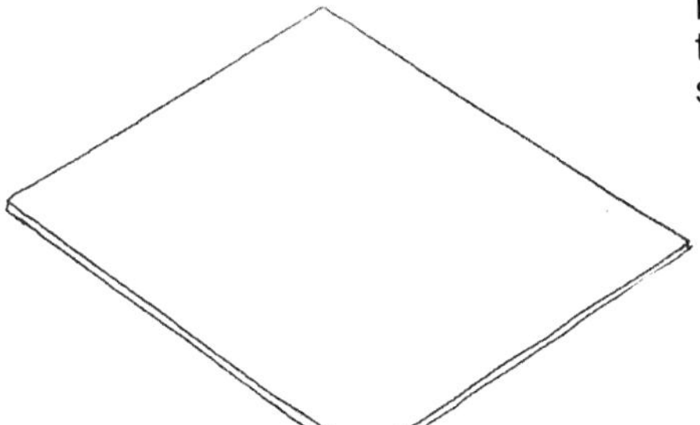

Round off the top with scissors.

Cut a piece of card 2cm wider than the width of two fingers.

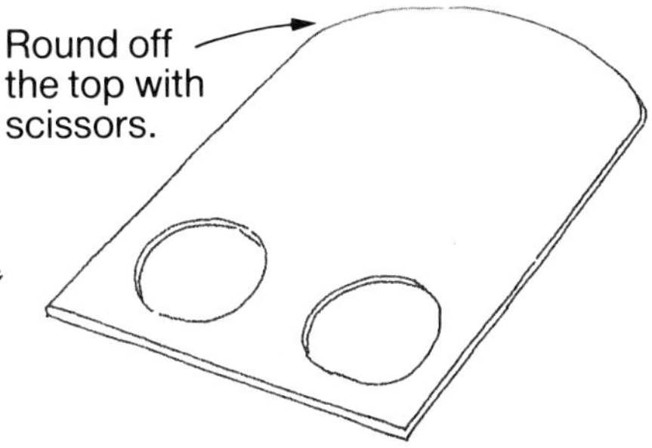

Make two holes near the bottom to poke your fingers through.

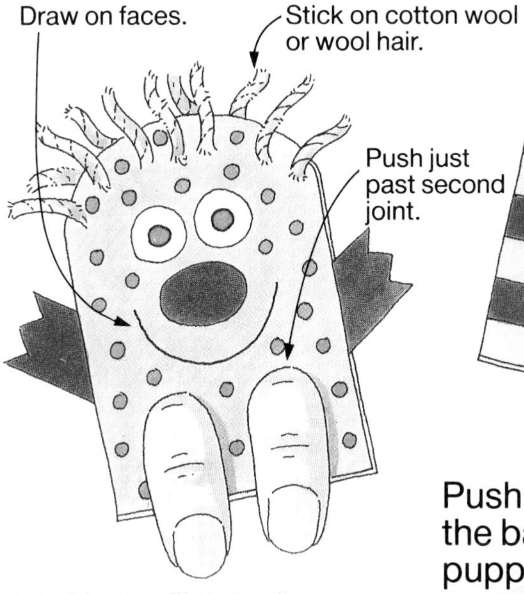

Draw on faces.

Stick on cotton wool or wool hair.

Push just past second joint.

Push your fingers through the back and make your puppet dance around.

Paper-bag puppets

Draw a face on one side of an upside down paper bag.

Twist the corners for ears. Put your hand in the bag and fix round your wrist with a rubber band.

Finger-end puppets

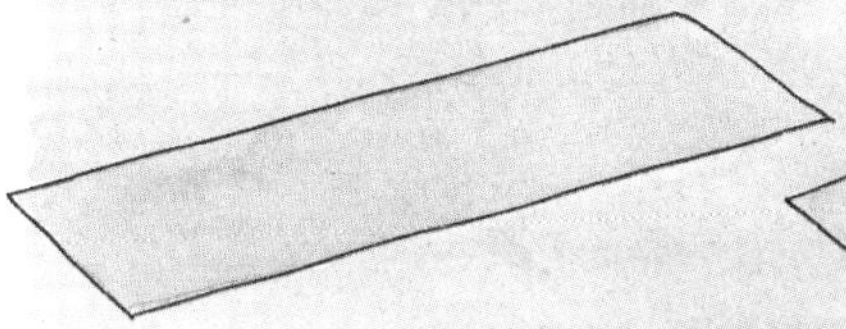

Cut strips of paper about 2cm wide by 5cm long.

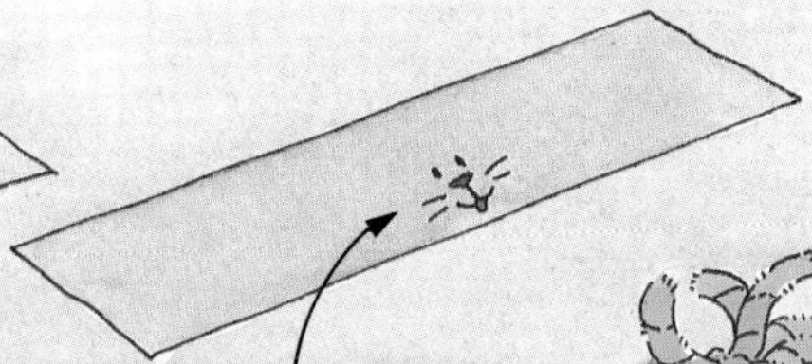

Draw a face in the centre of each strip.

Bend the strips round the ends of your fingers and stick to fit.

Add some hair.

Add some ears.

51

Costumes and disguises

You will need:

 paper plates (18cms diameter)
 pencil
round-ended scissors
felt-tip pen
 yoghurt carton
 sticky tape or glue
wool
doily

Mr Wolf mask

Cut holes for your eyes and a space for your nose, in a paper plate.

Cut a section from a yoghurt pot, as shown.

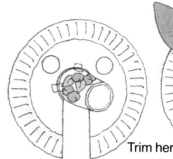

Tape or glue the yoghurt pot onto the plate, cut side downwards.

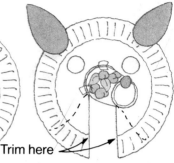

Trim here

Add ears and a nose cut from stiff paper. Trim away sharp edges, so you can speak easily.

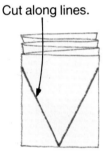

Cut along lines.

Fold some paper as shown and cut along lines to make teeth.

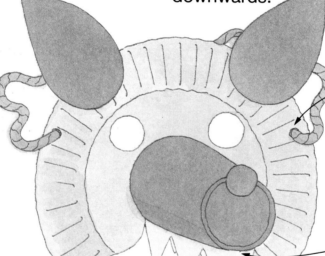

Poke holes at sides of plate and fix wool or elastic through.

Paint the mask if you like.

Stick teeth around cut section of yoghurt pot.

Other masks to try

The three little pigs
Cut a yoghurt pot down to make a snout. Stick on as for the wolf. Draw in nostrils and paint. Add ears. Trim the sharp edges.

Goldilocks and the three bears
Cut the centre out of a doily to make a lace collar for Goldilocks.

Make the bears' ears round. Stick on noses. Trim sharp edges.

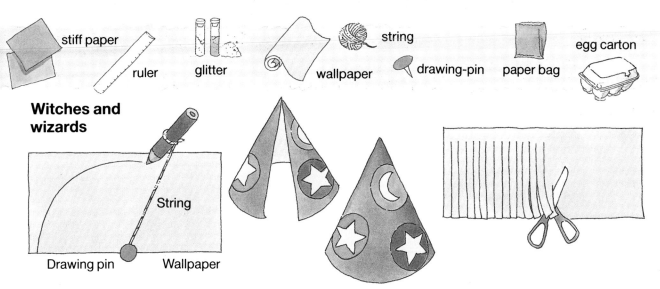

stiff paper
ruler
glitter
wallpaper
string
drawing-pin
paper bag
egg carton

Witches and wizards

String

Drawing pin   Wallpaper

For a hat draw a semicircle by tying string to a pencil and drawing an arc. Cut along the line.

Stick the edges together to fit your head size. Paint and decorate.

For hair, snip a band of paper and stick inside the hat.

To make a star draw two overlapping triangles, then cut round their outer lines. Spread glue on the star and sprinkle glitter over it. Shake off the excess glitter, then stick on the end of a plastic ruler.

Cut long nails from folded paper and tape onto finger ends.

Other fancy dress ideas

Posh woman
Make a tiara by folding a doily in half. Stick on crumpled sweetpapers or tinfoil for jewels. Use hairclips to fasten onto head.

Posh man
Draw a big bow-tie, colour it and cut it out. Pin it onto clothes.

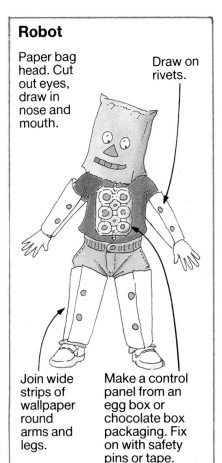

Robot

Paper bag head. Cut out eyes, draw in nose and mouth.

Draw on rivets.

Join wide strips of wallpaper round arms and legs.

Make a control panel from an egg box or chocolate box packaging. Fix on with safety pins or tape.

Surprise doors

You will need: two large sheets of wallpaper · non-fungicidal wallpaper paste · large paste-brush · round-ended scissors · felt-tip pens or paints

On a big piece of paper draw a large castle or house, with plenty of doors and windows.

Cut round the doors and windows, so they will open and shut.

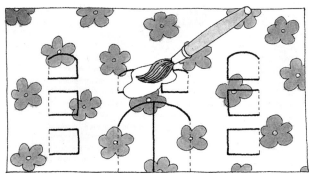

Cover the back of the picture, except the doors and windows, with paste. Stick it down onto the white side of another piece of wallpaper. Leave it to dry.

Open up the doors and windows so you can draw what's going on inside. Make up a story about it.

Other ideas to try

Kitchen
Make a kitchen with fridge, cupboards, washing machine and freezer.

Show what is inside each of them.

Ship
Make a ship with big portholes that will open and shut.

Show what the sailors, passengers and captain are all doing.,

54

Family portrait book

You will need: wallpaper or sugar paper ⬩ glue ⬩ round-ended scissors ⬩ felt-tip pens ⬩ white drawing paper

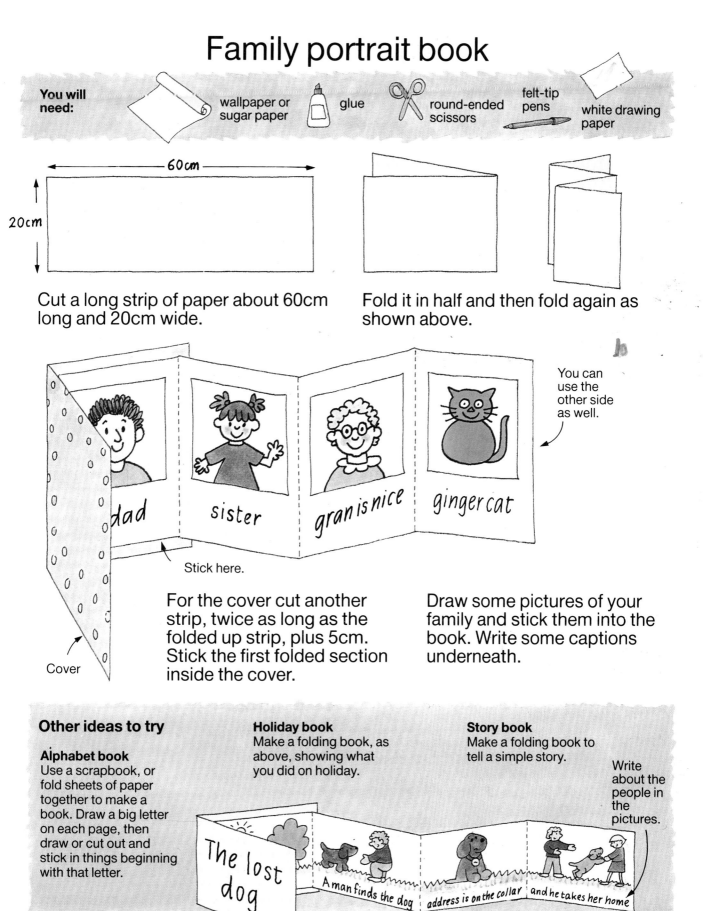

Cut a long strip of paper about 60cm long and 20cm wide.

Fold it in half and then fold again as shown above.

You can use the other side as well.

Stick here.

Cover

For the cover cut another strip, twice as long as the folded up strip, plus 5cm. Stick the first folded section inside the cover.

Draw some pictures of your family and stick them into the book. Write some captions underneath.

dad   sister   gran is nice   ginger cat

Other ideas to try

Alphabet book
Use a scrapbook, or fold sheets of paper together to make a book. Draw a big letter on each page, then draw or cut out and stick in things beginning with that letter.

Holiday book
Make a folding book, as above, showing what you did on holiday.

Story book
Make a folding book to tell a simple story.

Write about the people in the pictures.

The lost dog   A man finds the dog   address is on the collar   and he takes her home

55

Jewellery

You will need: wrapping paper or other colourful paper   paper glue   wool or fine elastic   large blunt needle   crochet hook or hair clip   felt-tip pens   straw   pencil

Straw beads

Cut strips of patterned paper the length of a straw and about 8cm wide. Cover them with glue on the plain side.

Lay a straw on one long edge and roll the paper round it as firmly as you can. Leave to dry. Repeat this process several times.

Cut the straw beads into any length you like. If the ends flatten squeeze them into round shapes again.

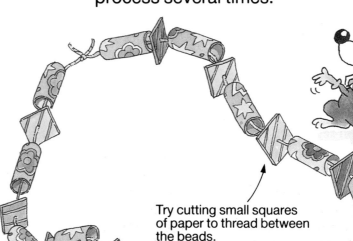

Try cutting small squares of paper to thread between the beads.

If you have no wrapping paper, colour some white paper yourself, or use pages from an old magazine or catalogue.

Brooches

Draw or cut out pictures you like to stick onto cereal-box card.

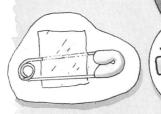

Attach a safety pin at the back with tape to make a brooch.

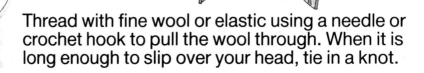

Thread with fine wool or elastic using a needle or crochet hook to pull the wool through. When it is long enough to slip over your head, tie in a knot.

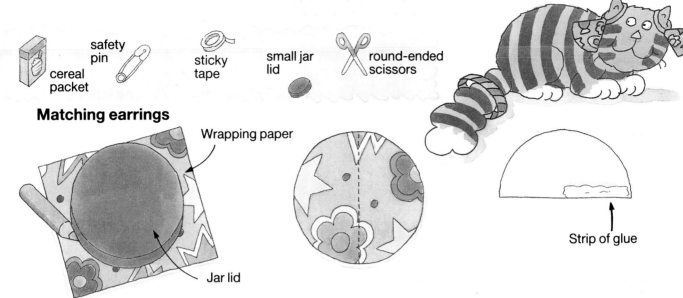

cereal
packet

safety
pin

sticky
tape

small jar
lid

round-ended
scissors

Matching earrings

Wrapping paper

Jar lid

Strip of glue

Draw round a small jar
lid to make a circle. Cut
the circle out.

Fold the circle in half,
then cut along the
fold line.

Put a strip of glue
halfway along each
straight edge on the
wrong side.

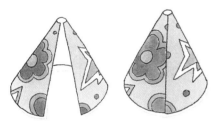

Bend round and
overlap the edges to
make a cone. Stick
down firmly. Snip the
top off the cone.

Loop some
wool through
the cone using
a crochet
hook or hair
clip to help you
thread it through.

Stick the
ends inside
the cone,
leaving the
loops to
hang over
your ears.

Ideas for bracelets

Cut two strips of different-coloured paper, one to fit round your wrist
and one much longer.

Wrap the long piece round the short piece to give a
striped effect. Join the ends with sticky tape to make
a circle. Glue down the ends and trim.

Make a long concertina shape,
by folding two bits of paper
across each other at right
angles. Stick into a circle.

Make a bracelet using straw
beads threaded onto string or
elastic.

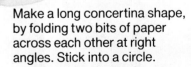

57

Greetings cards

You will need: white paper  stiff, coloured paper felt-tip pens or crayons  round-ended scissors

Pop-up cards

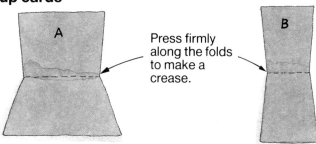

Press firmly along the folds to make a crease.

Put glue on this side.

Cut an oblong piece of paper (A) and fold the longest sides in half.

Cut a strip (B) about 3cms wide and half the length of A. Fold in half.

Open it out, turn it over, fold each end up about 1cm. Glue each end.

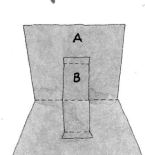

Lift the top half of A towards you so that B stands out.

When you open the card the picture will pop up.

Lay B down the centre of A, glue side down, so that the creases exactly correspond.

Colour and cut out a picture to cover the lower half of B. Stick it on.

Write your message here.

Name cards

Make an oblong card long enough to write your chosen name in big letters. Write the name onto it.

Stick little pieces of screwed-up sweet wrappers or tissue over the letters you have drawn. You can also make them into patterns.

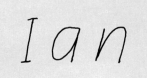

58

glue

tissue paper
or sweetpapers

old photos

paper
fasteners
ruler

Contrast cards

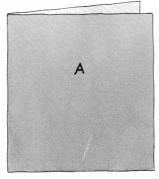

A

Fold an oblong piece
of paper in half to
make a card (A).

B

Cut another piece (B),
half the width of the
front, in a different
colour.

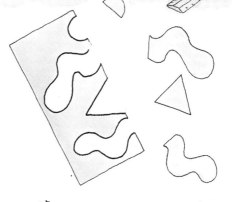

Cut deep shapes from
the right-hand side of
(B). Save all the pieces
you have cut.

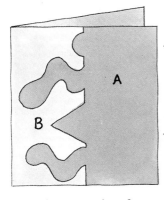

A

B

Stick (B) onto the front
left half of (A).

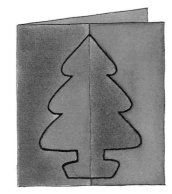

Turn over the cut-out pieces and stick them down
opposite the corresponding shapes, so that they
mirror each other.

Other ideas for cards

Paper fastener cards
Use paper fasteners to fix
separate parts, such as ears or
wheels onto your cards. Poke
the holes first with a pencil.

Photo cards
Cut some faces of your family
from unwanted photos. They
can be quite small.

Stick them onto a card, then
draw a picture round them.

59

Paper presents

You will need:  paper  felt-tip pens 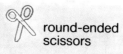 round-ended scissors  old magazines glue

Hand bookmark

Draw round your hand with a felt-tip pen.

Colour the hand brightly.

Cut it out carefully.

Willy worm bookmark

Draw, colour and cut out a worm. He should be longer than the height of a book so that his head and tail will stick out.

Give your worm some clothes, or draw on things like glasses or a bowtie.

Stick onto a strip of paper and use it to put in a book so that the fingers show your place.

60

cereal box

sticky tape

clingfilm

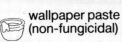
wallpaper paste (non-fungicidal)

wallpaper brush

yoghurt pot

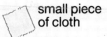
small piece of cloth

Mosaic place mat

Cut a large rectangle from a cereal box. Round off the corners with scissors.

Use a felt-tip pen to draw a big, bold design.

Find the colours you want to use in magazines. Tear them into pieces about 2cm square. Keep the colours separate.

Stick the coloured pieces onto the design.

Cover your dry mat with clingfilm taped on at the back.

Other ideas to try

Needle case
Fold a piece of stiff paper double to make a card. Draw a butterfly on it making sure the wings go right to the edge of the paper. Colour or decorate brightly and cut out double, so that it opens out.

Glue a small piece of cloth at the top only and stick onto the right side, for keeping needles in.

Write or copy your message on the left.

Pencil holder
Cover a yoghurt pot or cut-down plastic bottle with paper from an old comic or toy catalogue.

Hints

It is easier to paste the mat than the small bits of paper.

The more shades of each colour you use, the better the result.

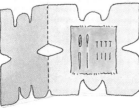

Paper bowls

You will need:

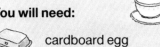 cardboard egg carton

cereal bowl and plate*

clingfilm

electric food mixer

old tea towel

round-ended scissors

sieve

large bowl

Tear the egg box into pieces and soak in warm water in a large bowl until soft (10-20 mins.).

If you haven't got a mixer, squash the pieces up with your hands.

Tip some of the water into the food mixer. Switch it on and add the pieces gradually until you have a watery, mushy pulp.

Tip the mixture into a fine-mesh sieve over the sink. Press down to squeeze out most of the water.

Cover the bowl completely.

Place the upturned cereal bowl onto a plate. Cover it with clingfilm. Press small lumps of paper pulp all over it.

Place the tea towel over the bowl and press firmly all over, to flatten the pulp and remove excess water.

Use oven gloves to take it out.

Leave to dry in a warm place, or put in a microwave oven* and cook on a high setting for 10-12 mins., or until it is dry.

When the pulp has dried, remove it from the cereal bowl and trim round the edge with some scissors.

Paint and decorate your bowl with poster paints.

Other ideas to try

Try using egg boxes of two or more different colours in your bowls.

To make a stronger bowl, try kneading a little non-fungicidal wallpaper paste into the pulp after sieving.

*When using a microwave use only bowls and plates recommended for microwave use.

Materials and skills

The main equipment you will need to make the things shown in this book are paper, scissors, glue and felt-tip pens or paints. This page gives you advice on what type of glue, paper and scissors to use. The following page provides some tips and hints on cutting, folding and measuring.

The specific things you will need for each project are listed at the top of each page.

Scissors

All-plastic scissors can be fragile and not so good for use on stiffer papers or thin card. All-metal scissors can be heavy and awkward for children to use.

A good compromise is a pair of plastic scissors with a metal blade. These are often brightly-coloured and made in the shape of a bird, animal or fish.

Scissors should always be round-ended for safety and any adult's scissors should be put away out of reach immediately after use.

Glue

● Glue sticks are clean to use, with the gum easily directed to where you want it to go. Be sure to put the cap back after use. They can dry out quickly.

● Liquid glues and gums are useful and spread easily, but take longer to dry.

● P.V.A. (polyvinyl acetate) is good for sticking large areas. It is white but dries transparent. Protect clothing with aprons. Roll up sleeves. Wash brushes out carefully after use.

● Wallpaper paste is also good for large areas. It is very cheap and you can make up small batches as you need it. For safety always use the non-fungicidal type. If you have some left over, cover it with clingfilm and store in the fridge for use another day.

● Flour-and-water paste can be made up by making up a smooth paste, bringing to the boil and simmering for a few minutes. Make sure it is quite cool before use.

● Sticky tape is invaluable but can be tricky. Cut several strips and attach lightly at one end only to a suitable work-top edge ready for use.

Do not use solvent-based glues or instant bond glue.

Paper

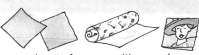

White paper – use sheets from a writing pad, typing paper, drawer or wall lining paper, or other similar paper.

Stiff paper – use wallpaper or the covers of magazines.

Strong paper – wallpaper is fairly strong.

Thin, strong paper – typing paper, or something similar.

Dark or coloured paper – sugar paper, paper from magazines or wrapping paper.

Card – use cut-up cereal boxes or something similar.

Collecting a supply of paper

You can collect most of the paper you need for these projects, without having to buy anything specially.

It is a good idea to keep a drawer or box in which to store all the odd bits you manage to find.

Below is a list of things it is worth saving.

● coloured foil or cellophane sweet wrappers

● clear cellophane from flowers and boxes of pasta

● tissue paper from fruit or packaging

● thin card from cereal boxes and the packaging in shirts or tights

● brightly-coloured pages from glossy magazines, leaflets or comics

● out-of-date catalogues

● corrugated paper is often used to pack china

● wrapping paper from birthdays or Christmas

● wallpaper is invaluable for its pattern value and strength and for its possibilities as drawing or painting paper

Materials and skills

Other good things to have

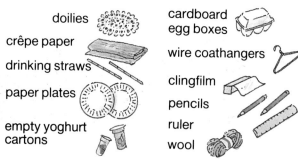

doilies

crêpe paper

drinking straws

paper plates

empty yoghurt cartons

cardboard egg boxes

wire coathangers

clingfilm

pencils

ruler

wool

Folding paper

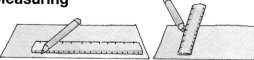

Folding is often repetitive, so you could do one fold and let your child copy you.

Point out before each step which edge is to be lined up with which. Show your child how to hold them firmly down while pressing in the crease.

Encourage her to check each time that the result looks like the drawing.

Measuring

Making things from paper provides good opportunities for learning about measuring.

You will probably need to do any accurate measuring required yourself, but your child can learn a lot from watching you, especially if you explain carefully what you are doing.

When she is ready to try measuring for herself, show her how to line the ruler up accurately and mark off the required length with a pencil.

Using scissors

This may take a little time for a child to master. To begin with she could be encouraged to cut along straight lines. Let her draw some herself on newspaper, using a ruler. She could then progress to curved lines. Draw round a dinner plate to start with, then progress to a tea plate, where the curve will be sharper and so on.

On larger projects take it in turns to do the cutting. As she becomes ready for them, show your child the techniques explained in the next column.

Cutting round a shape

●Always cut a rough outline first, this takes away an unmanageable mass of paper.

●Encourage your child to hold the paper lightly with her free hand near to where she will cut, to avoid tearing.

●Explain that she should not pull on the paper, the scissors should do the work.

●Demonstrate how to line up the blades of the scissors along the line to be cut to make it as accurate as possible.

Cutting out a shape

●Poke a hole in the centre of the shape to be removed with the pointed end of a pencil.

●Insert the lower blade of the scissors into the hole and cut to the edge of the shape.

●Cut round it carefully and remove it.

●If the paper is too stiff cut a slit in the paper by bending, rather than creasing the paper in the centre of the unwanted area. Make a cut into the folded edge, open out and insert the scissors. Cut to the edge.

ODDS & ENDS

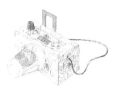

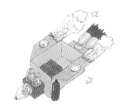

There is a great variety of things you can make using odds and ends from around the house. This book is designed to give you some ideas and starting points. Besides providing enjoyment and satisfaction, this type of activity can help young children to develop skills such as hand control and co-ordination, concentration and decision-making, and broaden their understanding of concepts such as size, shape, space and measurement.

Post box

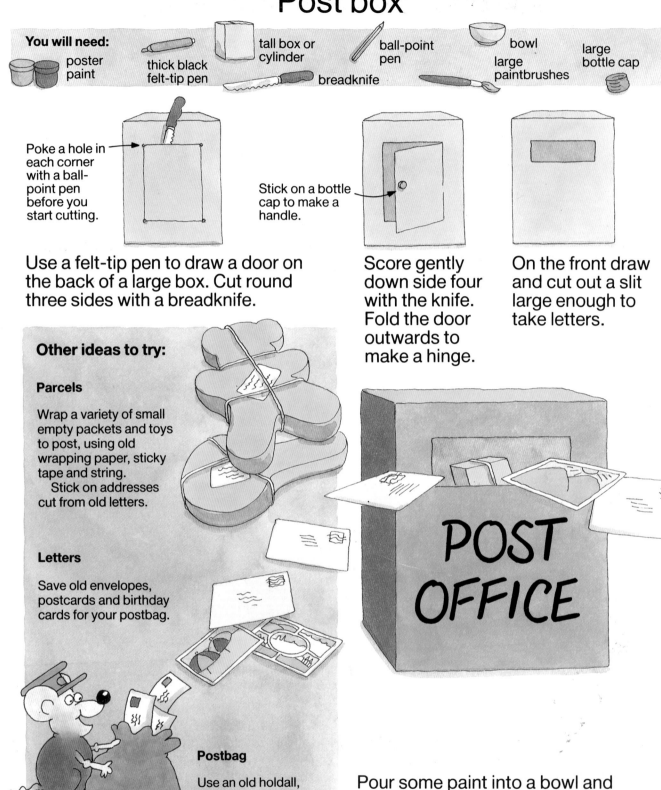

You will need:
poster paint · thick black felt-tip pen · tall box or cylinder · ball-point pen · breadknife · bowl · large paintbrushes · large bottle cap

Poke a hole in each corner with a ball-point pen before you start cutting.

Stick on a bottle cap to make a handle.

Use a felt-tip pen to draw a door on the back of a large box. Cut round three sides with a breadknife.

Score gently down side four with the knife. Fold the door outwards to make a hinge.

On the front draw and cut out a slit large enough to take letters.

Other ideas to try:

Parcels

Wrap a variety of small empty packets and toys to post, using old wrapping paper, sticky tape and string.
Stick on addresses cut from old letters.

Letters

Save old envelopes, postcards and birthday cards for your postbag.

Postbag

Use an old holdall, shopping bag or big shoulder bag.

POST OFFICE

Pour some paint into a bowl and paint the box. When the paint has dried add patterns and a label using felt-tip pen.

Ink-pad and franking stamp

You will need: scissors 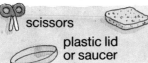 thin kitchen sponge (about 4cm by 4cm) glue

 screw-top bottle cap   plastic lid or saucer   elastic band   poster paint

 Trim away any excess with scissors.

Spread glue over the bottle top as shown above.

Lay pieces of elastic band onto the glue.

Place a piece of damp sponge in the plastic lid.

Pour a little paint into the centre of the sponge.

Press the bottle top into the paint and print firmly over the stamps (see right).

Stamps

Use an unthreaded sewing machine to perforate squares of gummed paper. Draw a simple design on each stamp.

You could also use petrol coupon stamps.

Other ideas to try

Counter holder

Cut empty cereal boxes down to different heights. Glue them together in order of size. Stock with postcards, licences and birthday cards to sell.

Add a cardboard tube for holding pens and pencils.

Cash box and money

Use a plastic ice cream box to hold toy money.

Make your own money by cutting notes out of paper.

For coins use washed and flattened foil bottle tops.

Add a toy telephone and some kitchen scales on which to weigh parcels.

Camera and photos

You will need: scissors glue 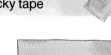 large toothpaste cap small plastic carton or cup

 small hinge-lid box (e.g. tea-bag box)

ball-point pen

75cm wool or plastic packaging tape

pictures cut from magazines or newspapers, or squares of plain paper

sticky tape

piece of thin card (4cm by 5cm)

piece of clingfilm (4cm by 5cm)

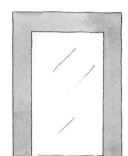

Assemble your camera as shown below.

For a press button glue a toothpaste cap to the top of the box.

Glue the viewfinder to the top back of the box.

To make the viewfinder, cut out the centre of a piece of card, as shown. Stick the clingfilm over it, then glue it to the top of the box.

Use a ball-point pen to poke holes in either side of the box for a strap. Thread the tape or wool through and knot on the inside.

Have the hinge of the lid at the top front of the box.

Hints

If you use wool for the strap, you can stiffen the ends with sticky tape to make it easier to thread through the holes.

Remember to take into account whether the photographer is right or left-handed before sticking on the press button.

Glue the plastic carton or cup to the centre front of the box to look like a lens.

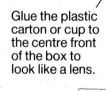

Photographs

Cut small pictures from magazines or newspapers, or draw some pictures on squares of paper.
Keep the "photographs" inside the box.

Binoculars

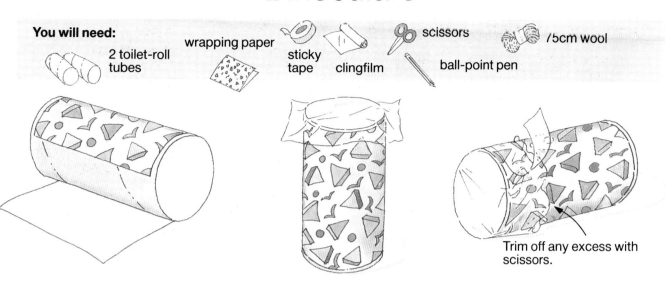

You will need:
2 toilet-roll tubes
wrapping paper
sticky tape
scissors
clingfilm
ball-point pen
75cm wool

Trim off any excess with scissors.

Cut a piece of wrapping paper to cover each toilet-roll tube. Secure it with sticky tape.

Cut a piece of clingfilm to cover the ends of each toilet-roll tube. Use sticky tape to hold it in place.

Use a ball-point pen to poke two holes for the straps.

Thread wool through the holes. Tie knots in the ends to secure it.

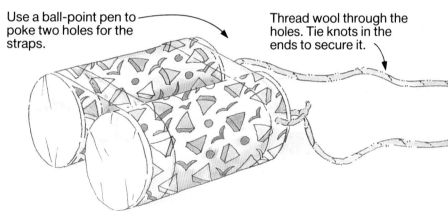

Stick the tubes firmly together using two strips of sticky tape.

Hints

If you have no toilet-roll tubes cut up a kitchen-roll tube using a breadknife as a saw.

When using sticky tape cut the required number of strips and attach them lightly to your work surface ready for use.

Use microwave clingfilm for easier handling.

Other ideas to try

Walkie-talkie

Wrap a 250ml juice carton in paper, as you would wrap a small parcel. Use a straw as an aerial.
 Stick on squares of gummed paper for buttons and write numbers on them.

Coloured flashlight

Change the colour of a torch beam by securing coloured cellophane over the glass with an elastic band.

Magic telescope

Stick coloured cellophane over a kitchen-roll tube, so that everything looks a different colour.

Moon rocket

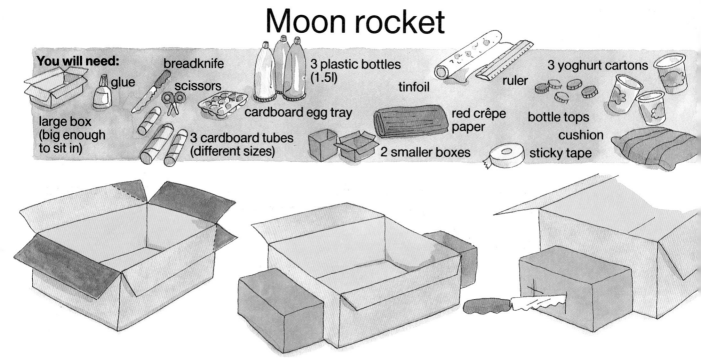

You will need: glue, breadknife, scissors, large box (big enough to sit in), 3 cardboard tubes (different sizes), cardboard egg tray, 3 plastic bottles (1.5l), tinfoil, 2 smaller boxes, red crêpe paper, ruler, 3 yoghurt cartons, bottle tops, cushion, sticky tape

Using a breadknife, cut off the parts of the large box shaded dark brown in the picture above.

Use glue and sticky tape to fix the smaller boxes to the front and back, to make a nose and a fuel tank.

Cut two crosses 4cm by 4cm in the back of the fuel tank, using the tip of the breadknife.

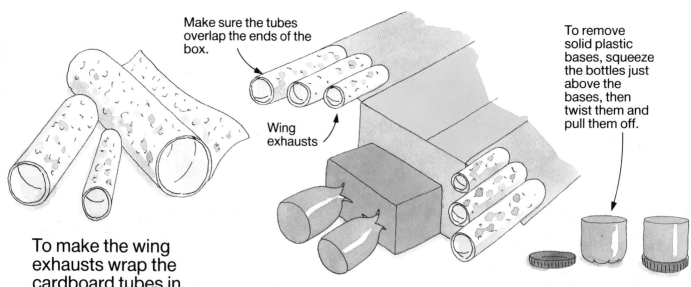

Make sure the tubes overlap the ends of the box.

Wing exhausts

To remove solid plastic bases, squeeze the bottles just above the bases, then twist them and pull them off.

To make the wing exhausts wrap the cardboard tubes in tinfoil, securing it with sticky tape. Cut each tube in half. Stick the tubes onto the wings.

To make the tail exhausts, cut the bottoms off the bottles about 9cm from the base. Insert two of the bottle necks firmly into the crosses cut in the fuel tank. You will need the bases later.

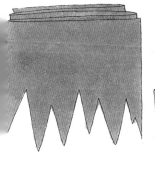 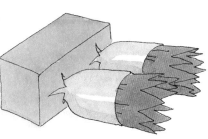  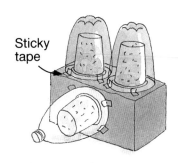

Sticky tape

Fold a piece of crêpe paper and cut a jagged edge so that it looks like flames. Cut it into two pieces. Roll each piece loosely and bunch it into the bottles. Secure it with sticky tape.

For lights, cover yoghurt pots with tinfoil. Glue two pots on top of the nose and a third on the front.

Fix the remaining cut bottle and two bottle bases over them with sticky tape.

Control panel

Cover an egg tray with tinfoil, pressing gently into the hollows.

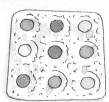

Glue bottle tops in the hollows to make press buttons.

Fix the panel to the inside front of the spaceship.

Add a cushion for the pilot to sit on.

Use an empty washing-liquid container as a can for spare fuel.

Hints

If you don't have all the things listed, you can easily improvise on the basic shape with such things as jar lids, polystyrene packaging and plastic food trays.

For a larger spaceship stick a second box between the main body and the fuel tank.

For extra decoration cover the solid plastic bottle bases with foil and stick them onto the wings and fuel tank.

71

Caravan

You will need: very large box (for fridge, cooker or something similar) breadknife large, thin book felt-tip pen large bottle cap sticky tape ruler scissors

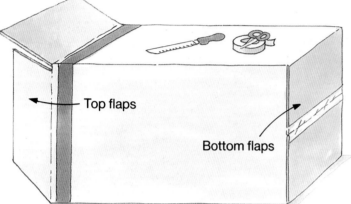

Top flaps

Bottom flaps

Lay the box on its side and cut off any top flaps, using a breadknife. Use sticky tape to close the bottom flaps firmly.

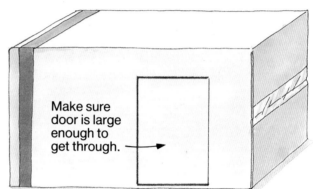

Make sure door is large enough to get through.

Using a ruler, draw a door shape large enough for your child to get through. Cut round three sides and bend it outwards to make a door.

Cut a tab 5cm by 10cm and glue it onto the sunroof to make a latch.

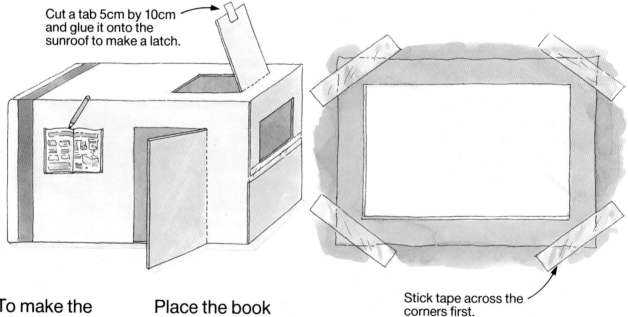

Stick tape across the corners first.

To make the windows draw round a thin, open book, then cut round the lines with a breadknife.

Place the book on the roof and draw round it. Cut round three sides and bend the flap up to make a sunroof.

Cut pieces of clingfilm larger than the open book and use sticky tape to fix them over the inside of the windows.

72

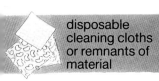
disposable
cleaning cloths
or remnants of
material

glue

clingfilm

4 paper plates
or plastic lids

Other ideas to try:

Make a small caravan for a doll
or teddy. Choose a box it can fit
inside.

Make a tiny caravan from a very
small box. Attach it to a toy car,
using string or sticky tape.

Make folds
along the top of
the material.

Cut strips of material and
use sticky tape to fix them
to the top inside edges of
the windows for curtains.

Put a small box inside
to make a table and a
cushion for a seat. Add
a torch, plastic cups
and a drink in a plastic
bottle.

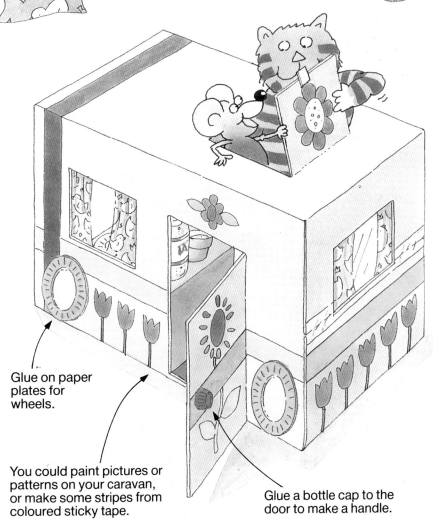

Glue on paper
plates for
wheels.

Hint

Turn the box so whichever
side you are working on is
at the top.

You could paint pictures or
patterns on your caravan,
or make some stripes from
coloured sticky tape.

Glue a bottle cap to the
door to make a handle.

Airport and heliport

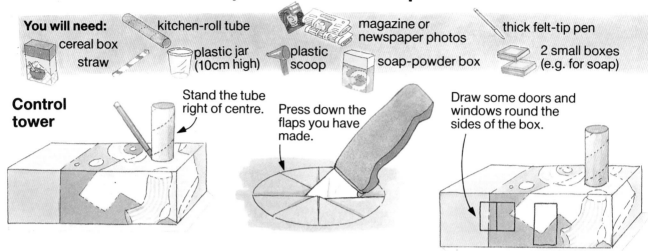

You will need: cereal box, straw, kitchen-roll tube, plastic jar (10cm high), plastic scoop, magazine or newspaper photos, soap-powder box, thick felt-tip pen, 2 small boxes (e.g. for soap)

Control tower

Stand the tube right of centre.

Press down the flaps you have made.

Draw some doors and windows round the sides of the box.

Stand the kitchen-roll tube on the soap-powder box, as shown, and draw round it with a felt-tip pen.

Poke a slit in the centre of the circle. Cut to the edge, using a breadknife. Make cuts all the way round, as shown.

Push the kitchen roll firmly into the hole so that it stands upright.

If you have not got a plastic jar, use a breadknife to cut down a clear, plastic bottle.

Helicopter pad

Cut some pictures of people from magazine photographs. Glue them onto the inside of the upturned plastic jar.

Put plenty of glue round the top of the kitchen-roll tube. Press the plastic jar firmly on top.

Remove the lid from a pizza box and turn the box upside down.
Draw round a jar lid to make a large circle in the centre. Write a large "H" for helicopter in the circle.

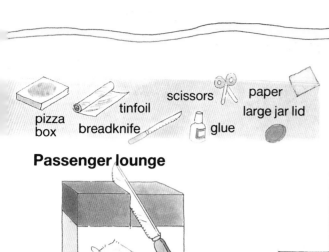

pizza box · tinfoil · scissors · paper · large jar lid · breadknife · glue

Passenger lounge

Saw a cereal box in half lengthways, using a breadknife. Turn one half on its side and glue it onto the left of the control tower base.

Stick a small box on top of it to make a look-out point. Make a hole in the small box, push in a straw and stick on a paper flag.

Car park

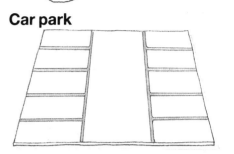

Remove the flaps from the pizza box lid. Draw car spaces on the lid and put it in front of the control tower.

Radar

Push the handle of a scoop into a small box and glue the box to the top of the control tower building.

Runway

Using scissors, cut away the side panel from the remaining half of the cereal box. Open out the box to make a flat strip.

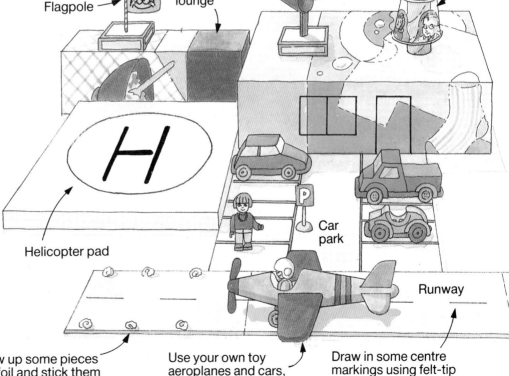

Flagpole · Passenger lounge · Radar · Control tower

Helicopter pad

Car park

Runway

Screw up some pieces of tinfoil and stick them down the edges of the runway for lights.

Use your own toy aeroplanes and cars, plastic figures and traffic signs.

Draw in some centre markings using felt-tip pen.

Pull-along train

You will need:

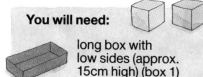 long box with low sides (approx. 15cm high) (box 1)

2 smaller boxes, narrower than box 1 (boxes 2 and 3)

 fat cardboard tube

 plastic tub

even smaller box (box 4)

sticky tape

glue

toilet-roll tube

 ruler

breadknife

ball-point pen

Engine base

Turn box 1 over to form a base. Using a ball-point pen, poke four holes, as shown above.

Cut a piece of washing line about 120cm long. Poke the ends through the top holes and knot them inside the box.

Cut another piece of washing line about 70cm long. Thread it through the back holes and leave the ends free.

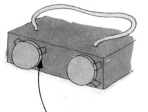

Hold in place with sticky tape.

Glue the jar lids onto the front to make buffers.

Cabin

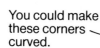

You could make these corners curved.

On box 2, draw lines as shown above, using a ruler and a felt-tip pen. Cut along the lines with a breadknife.

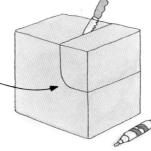

Using a plastic tub as a template, draw a circle in the top front left-hand corner. Make a hole in the centre of the circle, using a ball-point pen.

Insert the breadknife, cut to the edge, then round the outline of the circle. Remove the circle to make a window for the driver.

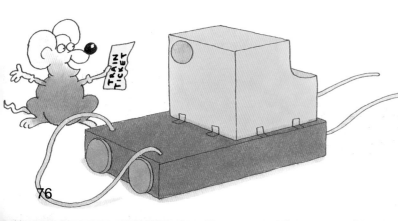

Glue the cabin to the back end of the base. Use sticky tape for extra strength.

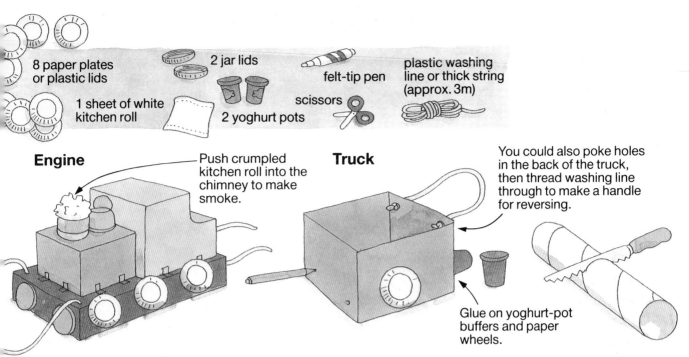

8 paper plates or plastic lids

1 sheet of white kitchen roll

2 jar lids

2 yoghurt pots

felt-tip pen

scissors

plastic washing line or thick string (approx. 3m)

Engine

Push crumpled kitchen roll into the chimney to make smoke.

Truck

You could also poke holes in the back of the truck, then thread washing line through to make a handle for reversing.

Glue on yoghurt-pot buffers and paper wheels.

Glue and tape box 4 in front of the cabin. Use sticky tape to fix the plastic tub and fat cardboard tube on top.

Glue three paper-plate wheels on each side.

In box 3, use a ball-point pen to make two holes to match the holes in the back of the engine base (box 1).

Cut a toilet-roll tube in half, using a breadknife.

You could paint your train or give it stripes made from coloured sticky tape.

Make a flag by sticking some red paper onto a garden cane.

Make some tickets by cutting up card or paper, or save old train tickets.

Hint

Make a longer train by adding another truck or a guard's van and attaching it in the same way.

Thread the pieces of tube onto the ends of the washing line at the back of the engine base. Then thread the ends through the holes at the front of the truck and tie them in a knot.

Dog kennel

You will need: ruler · ball-point pen · sticky tape · scissors · newspaper · flap-top box · breadknife · saucer · felt-tip pen · powder paint · corrugated cardboard · paintbrush

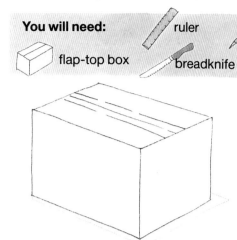

Stick the top flaps of the box down with tape. If necessary, do the same with the bottom flaps.

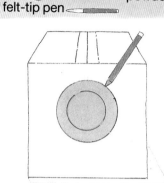

Place a saucer on the centre front of the box and draw round it with a felt-tip pen.

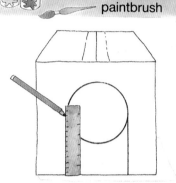

Using a ruler draw two lines from the sides of the circle to the bottom edge of the box.

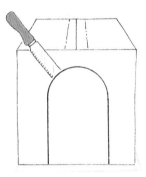

Using a breadknife cut round the arch-shape to make a doorway. To insert the knife, first make a hole with a ball-point pen.

Place the box on an old newspaper to paint it.

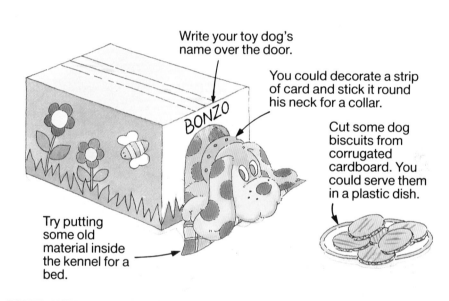

Write your toy dog's name over the door.

You could decorate a strip of card and stick it round his neck for a collar.

Cut some dog biscuits from corrugated cardboard. You could serve them in a plastic dish.

Try putting some old material inside the kennel for a bed.

Another idea to try
Cat basket

Using a ruler, draw a line round a box about 10cm from the base. Cut off the top using a breadknife.

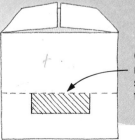

Cut a rectangular section from the front.

Paint the outside of the box and put a cushion inside for your toy cat to sit on.

Tying and threading trays

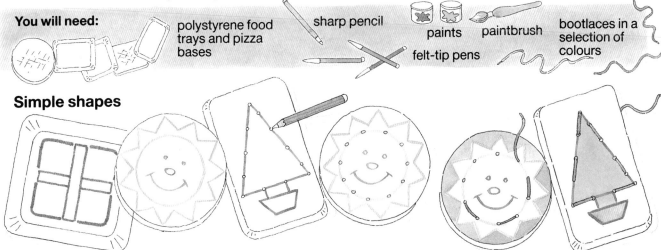

You will need: polystyrene food trays and pizza bases, sharp pencil, paints, paintbrush, felt-tip pens, bootlaces in a selection of colours

Simple shapes

Draw some large, simple shapes on the back of food trays, using felt-tip pens. You will need to press firmly.

Poke holes at intervals around the main outline, using a pencil with a sharp point.

Paint the shapes. Thread round the outline with laces.

Random patterns

Use a sharp pencil to poke holes through a food tray from the back.

If possible use several colours.

Use the tray for threading criss-cross patterns with bootlaces.

Shoe-laces

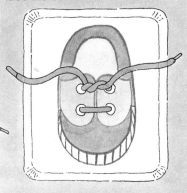

Draw and paint a shoe. Poke lace-holes in it.

Use the shoe to practise tying knots and bows.

Other ideas to try

Sewing on buttons

Use scissors to cut the bases off two clean, dry polystyrene cups about 1cm from the bottom.

Poke two holes in each, using a sharp pencil.

Draw and colour a clown on a food tray or a piece of card. Place the buttons on him and make four holes in the tray or card to correspond with the button holes.

"Sew" on the buttons with bootlaces.

79

Fleet of boats

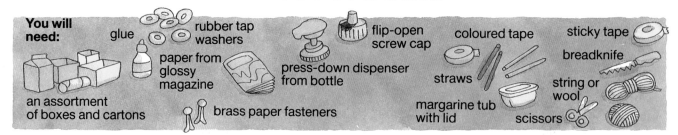

You will need: glue, rubber tap washers, paper from glossy magazine, press-down dispenser from bottle, flip-open screw cap, coloured tape, straws, margarine tub with lid, sticky tape, breadknife, string or wool, scissors, brass paper fasteners, an assortment of boxes and cartons

Police launch

Cut a clean dry milk carton in half lengthways.

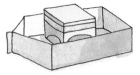

Cut down a light-bulb box and tape it into the centre of one half of the milk carton.

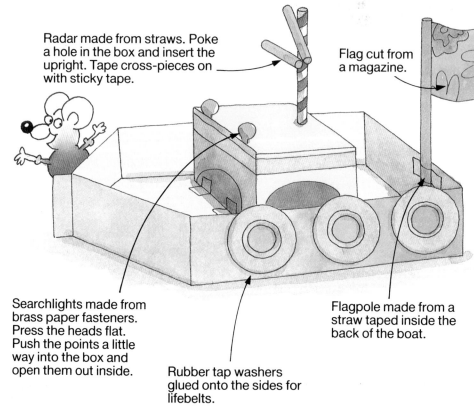

Radar made from straws. Poke a hole in the box and insert the upright. Tape cross-pieces on with sticky tape.

Flag cut from a magazine.

Searchlights made from brass paper fasteners. Press the heads flat. Push the points a little way into the box and open them out inside.

Rubber tap washers glued onto the sides for lifebelts.

Flagpole made from a straw taped inside the back of the boat.

Tugboat

Trim the bows slightly with scissors.

Glue a flat box (e.g. a sardine box) onto the base of a polystyrene food tray.

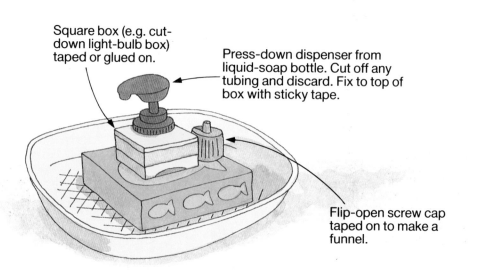

Square box (e.g. cut-down light-bulb box) taped or glued on.

Press-down dispenser from liquid-soap bottle. Cut off any tubing and discard. Fix to top of box with sticky tape.

Flip-open screw cap taped on to make a funnel.

Other ideas to try

Hovercraft

Fins cut from card, coloured and slotted into slits made with a breadknife.

Glue paper circles onto cut-down straws to make rotors.

Make holes with sharp scissors and push the straws in.

Upside-down margarine tub with lid.

Coloured tape

Catamaran

Magazine paper taped onto straw mast.

Sardine box

Toothpaste tube boxes.

Barges

Toilet-roll tube for cabin.

Long thin box (e.g. for biscuits)

Corks for cargo. You could also use twigs, matchboxes and raisin boxes.

Join the small barges to the big one by taping on string.

Matchbox centre

Bath-salt coal

Hints

Polystyrene packaging blocks make a good base for boats.

Assemble the cabins completely before sticking them to their bases.

Submarines

For submarines use shampoo bottles with various levels of water to float at different heights in the bath.

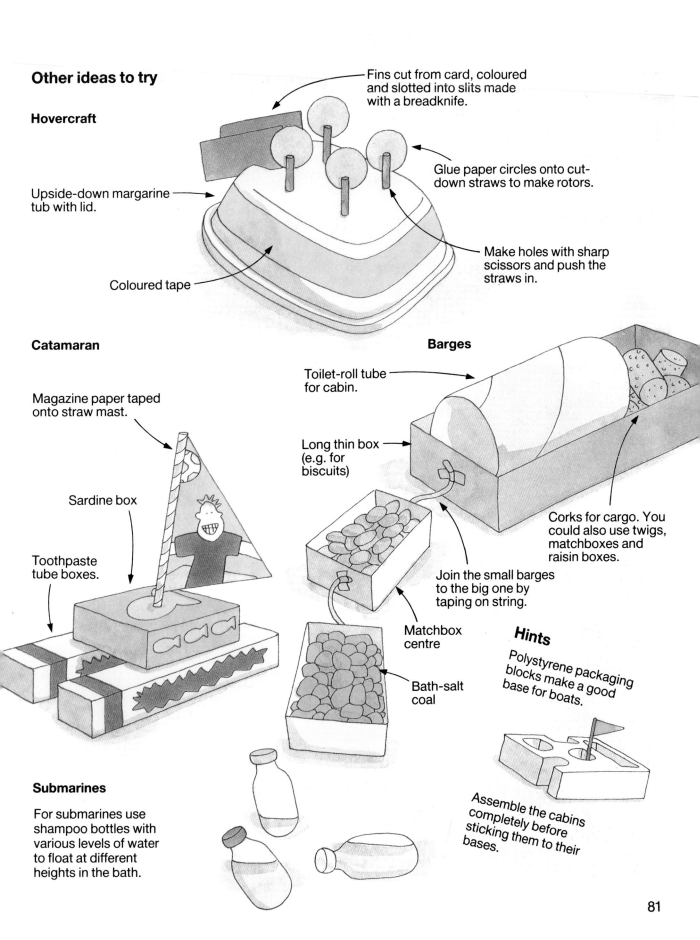

Cooker

You will need: breadknife, large screw-top bottle cap, glue, scissors, felt-tip pen, large box, ruler, tinfoil, 4 plastic tub or jar lids, 5 small bottle caps, sticky tape

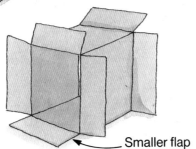

Smaller flap

Open up all the flaps on the box, as shown. Cut off the smaller, inside flaps, using a breadknife.

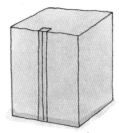

Tape the outer flaps firmly together at the top and the bottom.

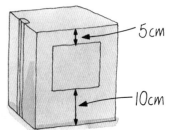

5cm

10cm

Draw a rectangle on the centre front of the box to make a door.

Using a breadknife, cut round three sides of the rectangle.

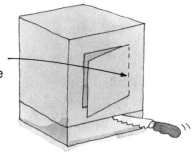

Fold back to make a hinge down the fourth side.

Using the breadknife, cut off the bottom 5cm of the box.

Turn this bottom piece upside down and trim a 1cm strip from the front.

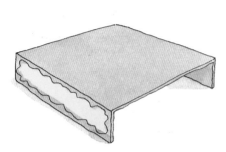

Put glue on the three sides that are left.

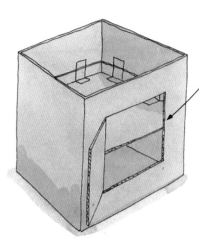

Make sure the trimmed edge of the shelf is at the front.

Turn the cooker upside down and push the glued piece firmly inside to form a shelf halfway down.
   Add sticky tape for extra support.

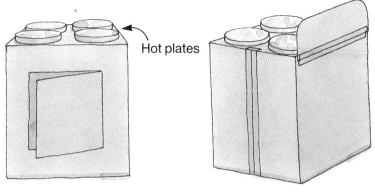
Hot plates

Cover jar lids with pieces of tinfoil and tape them to the top of the cooker.

Cut a strip of card 8cm deep, round off the top corners with scissors and tape it to the top back of the cooker.

To go with your cooker:

Use plastic margarine tubs as pans or mixing bowls.

Draw on a clock face.

Make food from playdough using a rolling pin and plastic cutters.

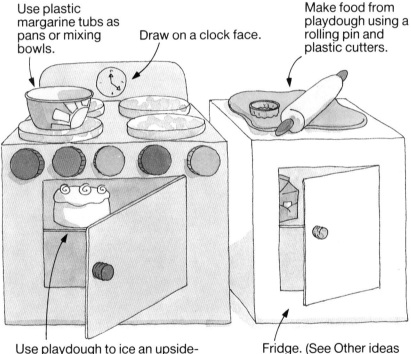

Use playdough to ice an upside-down margarine-tub cake on a paper plate. Add pasta shells as decoration.

Fridge. (See Other ideas to try, on the right.)

Glue and tape on bottle-cap knobs. Glue and tape on a screw-top door handle.

Other ideas to try

Fridge

Make as for the cooker, but leave out the hot plates and control knobs.

Fill with:

egg boxes

 empty, washed-out milk cartons

 playdough butter and cheese on paper plates or jar lids

crumpled tinfoil fish

 margarine and yoghurt tubs

Washing machine

Draw round a circular 1 litre ice cream tub on the centre front of a large box. Use a breadknife to cut almost round the circle, but leave a hinge at the side. Glue and tape the lid of the tub onto the door.

Cut a flap on top for soap powder.

Add a large screw-on bottle cap as the programming dial.

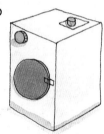

Borrow an apron and oven gloves from the kitchen.

Cut out some cardboard biscuits.

Use ice cream tub lids as baking trays.

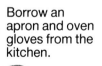

Teddy bear's bed

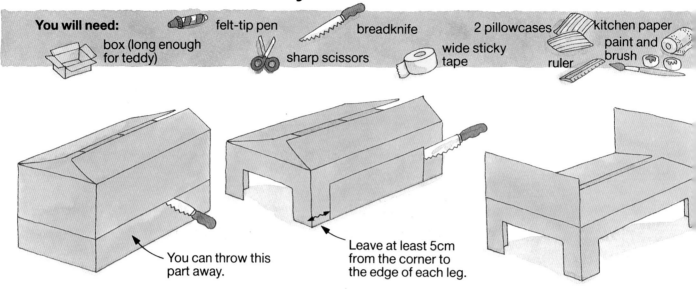

You will need: felt-tip pen, box (long enough for teddy), breadknife, sharp scissors, wide sticky tape, 2 pillowcases, ruler, kitchen paper, paint and brush

You can throw this part away.

Leave at least 5cm from the corner to the edge of each leg.

Place the box so you have the flaps at the top. Decide how high you want the bed, draw a line round the bottom and cut off the excess with a breadknife.

Draw and cut rectangular panels from each side, to give the bed four sturdy legs.

Open out the flaps. Fold the longest flaps back into place, leaving the end flaps free.

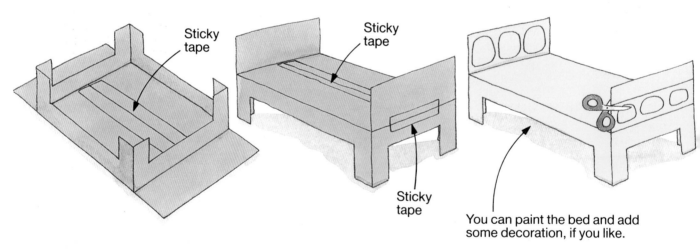

Sticky tape

Sticky tape

Sticky tape

You can paint the bed and add some decoration, if you like.

Turn the bed over and tape the long flaps securely into place underneath.

Turn it upright again and stick tape down the centre, and at each end to hold the end flaps upright.

Cut down one end flap to about two thirds of the height of the other and then round off the corners.

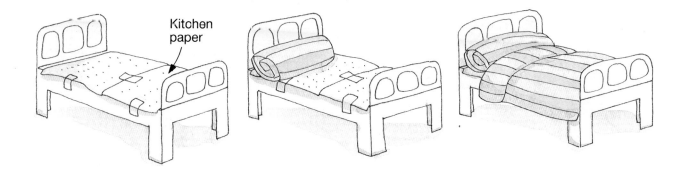

Use pieces of kitchen paper lightly taped onto the bed for a bottom sheet.

For the pillow, fold a pillowcase so that it fits the head end of the bed.

Use a second pillowcase as a blanket. Turn back the top.

Other idea to try

Hospital

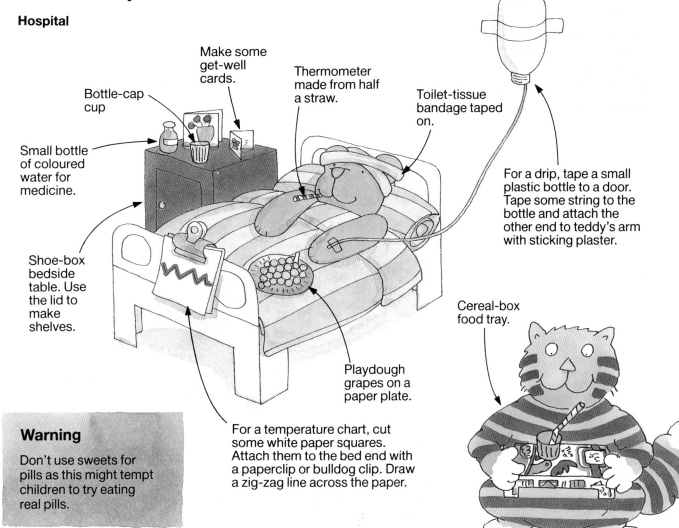

Make some get-well cards.

Bottle-cap cup

Thermometer made from half a straw.

Toilet-tissue bandage taped on.

Small bottle of coloured water for medicine.

For a drip, tape a small plastic bottle to a door. Tape some string to the bottle and attach the other end to teddy's arm with sticking plaster.

Shoe-box bedside table. Use the lid to make shelves.

Cereal-box food tray.

Playdough grapes on a paper plate.

For a temperature chart, cut some white paper squares. Attach them to the bed end with a paperclip or bulldog clip. Draw a zig-zag line across the paper.

Warning

Don't use sweets for pills as this might tempt children to try eating real pills.

Doll's playhouse

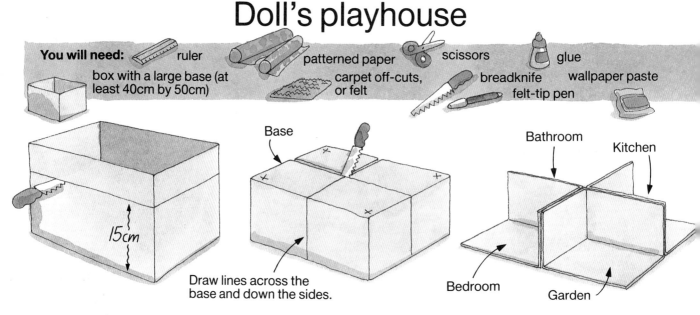

You will need: ruler · box with a large base (at least 40cm by 50cm) · patterned paper · carpet off-cuts, or felt · scissors · breadknife · felt-tip pen · glue · wallpaper paste

Draw lines across the base and down the sides.

Base

Bathroom · Kitchen · Bedroom · Garden

Using a ruler and a felt-tip, measure and mark a line all the way round the box, at least 15cm up from the base. Cut round the line with a breadknife.

Turn the box over and mark each corner with a cross. Measure and mark the box into quarters. Cut the box into four sections with a breadknife.

Keep the sections separate to decorate them. Then fit them together with the crosses in the centre underneath, long sides against long sides.

To paper your rooms

To carpet your rooms

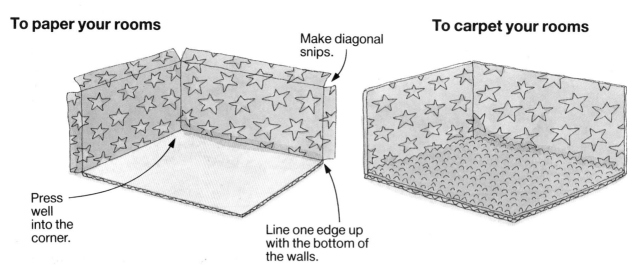

Make diagonal snips.

Press well into the corner.

Line one edge up with the bottom of the walls.

Cut a piece of paper longer and wider than the two walls of your room. Cover the back of the paper with wallpaper paste and stick it to the walls.

Make snips at the edges as shown. Fold the overlaps over and stick them down to make neat edges.

Trim carpet off-cuts or bits of felt, or patterned paper, to the right size. Stick them down with glue.

86

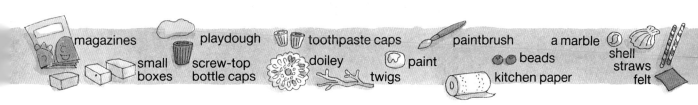

Here and on the next page are some ideas for decorating your rooms.

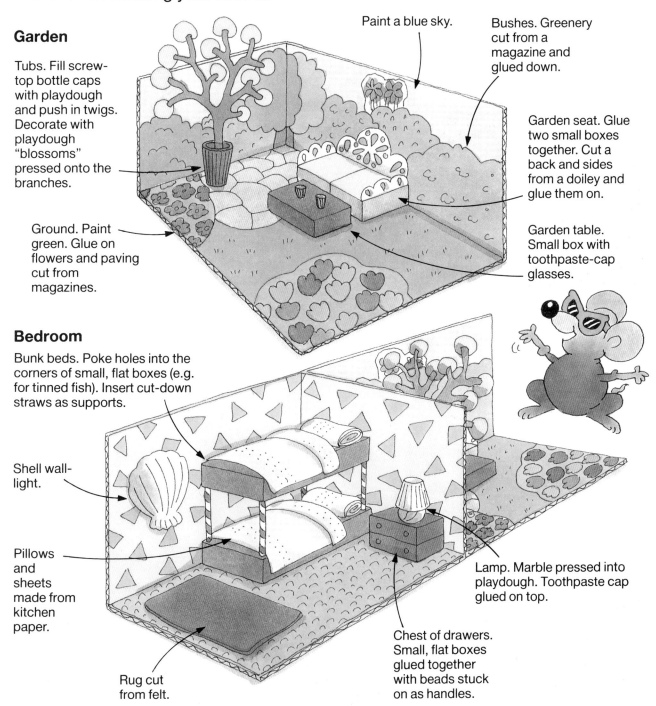

Garden

Tubs. Fill screw-top bottle caps with playdough and push in twigs. Decorate with playdough "blossoms" pressed onto the branches.

Ground. Paint green. Glue on flowers and paving cut from magazines.

Paint a blue sky.

Bushes. Greenery cut from a magazine and glued down.

Garden seat. Glue two small boxes together. Cut a back and sides from a doiley and glue them on.

Garden table. Small box with toothpaste-cap glasses.

Bedroom

Bunk beds. Poke holes into the corners of small, flat boxes (e.g. for tinned fish). Insert cut-down straws as supports.

Shell wall-light.

Pillows and sheets made from kitchen paper.

Rug cut from felt.

Lamp. Marble pressed into playdough. Toothpaste cap glued on top.

Chest of drawers. Small, flat boxes glued together with beads stuck on as handles.

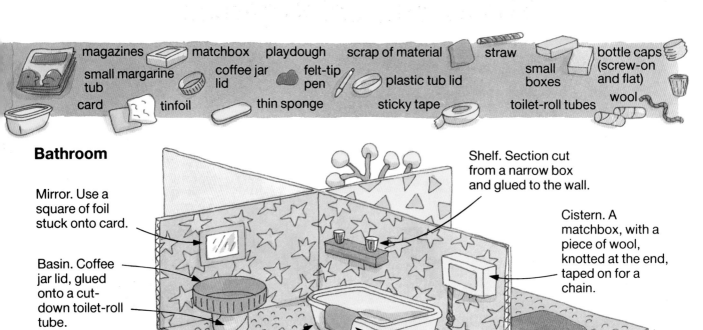

magazines matchbox playdough scrap of material straw bottle caps (screw-on and flat)

small margarine tub coffee jar lid felt-tip pen plastic tub lid small boxes

card tinfoil thin sponge sticky tape toilet-roll tubes wool

Bathroom

Mirror. Use a square of foil stuck onto card.

Basin. Coffee jar lid, glued onto a cut-down toilet-roll tube.

Bath. Small margarine tub.

Bathmat. Cut a piece from a thin sponge.

Shelf. Section cut from a narrow box and glued to the wall.

Cistern. A matchbox, with a piece of wool, knotted at the end, taped on for a chain.

Toilet. A screw-on bottle cap, with card taped on for a seat.

Towel. Scrap of material.

Kitchen

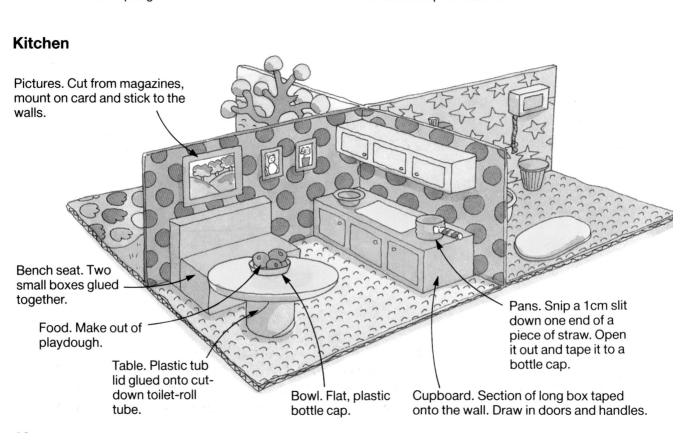

Pictures. Cut from magazines, mount on card and stick to the walls.

Bench seat. Two small boxes glued together.

Food. Make out of playdough.

Table. Plastic tub lid glued onto cut-down toilet-roll tube.

Bowl. Flat, plastic bottle cap.

Pans. Snip a 1cm slit down one end of a piece of straw. Open it out and tape it to a bottle cap.

Cupboard. Section of long box taped onto the wall. Draw in doors and handles.

88

Throw-and-catch games

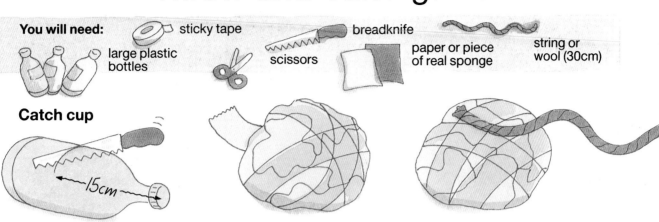

You will need: sticky tape · large plastic bottles · scissors · breadknife · paper or piece of real sponge · string or wool (30cm)

Catch cup

Using a breadknife, cut down a large plastic bottle.

Screw a piece of paper into a small ball. Wind sticky tape round it.

Tape a piece of string or wool, about 30cm long, to the ball.

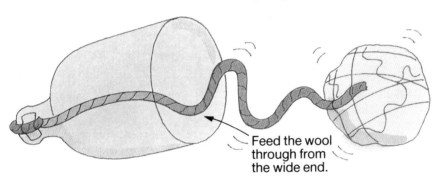

Feed the wool through from the wide end.

Remove the bottle cap. Feed the wool through the bottle and tape the end to the outside of the bottle neck.

Put the ball inside the bottle and then see how many times you can toss it up in the air and catch it again.

Bottle scoopers

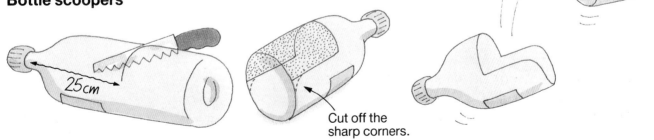

Cut off the sharp corners.

Cut down a large plastic bottle so that it measures about 25cm from the neck end.

Using scissors, cut out a section, as shown above. Round off the corners for safety.

Make another scoop and use them to throw and catch a paper ball between two people.

Guessing box

You will need: 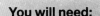 food tin (unopened) — kitchen cloth or other light material — felt-tip pen — scissors

 shoe box — ruler — sticky tape — breadknife — various small objects

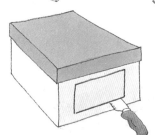

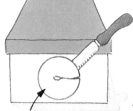

Make sure you can fit your hand inside.

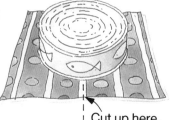

Cut up here.

Cut a rectangle out of one of the small sides of a shoe box.

Put a tin in the middle of the opposite end. Draw round it, using a felt-tip pen.

Push the point of a breadknife into the centre of the circle. Cut outwards to the edge and then round the circle.

Using the tin as a guide, cut a rectangle of material big enough to cover the circle easily. Cut it in half up the centre.

Tape along the top and down the sides.

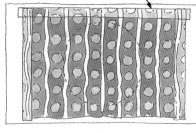

How to play

Tape the material to the inside of the box so that it covers the hole. Replace the box lid.

One person, the "chooser", chooses a variety of small objects, keeping them out of sight of the "guesser".

Hints

Try to vary the size, shape and texture of the objects as much as possible.

Don't use sharp or prickly objects.

Other ideas to try

Memory box

Put several things inside the box and remove the lid so the guesser can take a good look.

Put the lid back on, then remove one object without the guesser seeing.

Take the lid off again and see if the guesser can tell what's missing.

Tasting box

Put a variety of foods on saucers. The guesser dips a wet finger into each, in the box, and tastes it with their eyes closed.

The "chooser" puts one of the objects into the box through the rectangular hole. The "guesser" puts a hand through the material to feel the mystery object and tries to guess what it is.

Blow football

You will need: 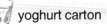 yoghurt carton green paint paint-brush felt-tip pen mug 2 straws

box or lid at least 30cm by 45cm sticky tape ruler scissors breadknife handful of dried peas

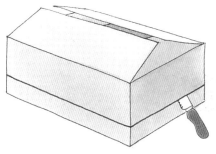

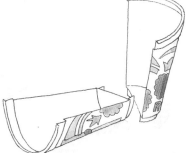

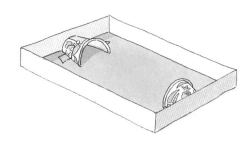

If you are using a box, cut round the base with a breadknife, 6cm from the bottom, to make a tray.

Cut a yoghurt pot in half, as shown above, using scissors.

Paint the pitch green. Tape the yoghurt pot halves at either end to make goals.

How to play

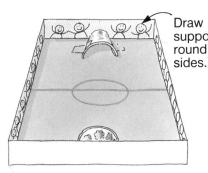

Draw supporters round the sides.

Draw a halfway line using a ruler and felt-tip pen. Draw round a mug to make a centre circle.

Put a handful of dried peas into the centre circle.

Each player has a straw and uses it to try to blow as many peas as possible into the opposite goal.

The game is over when all the peas are in goal. Count them to find out who is the winner.

Another idea to try

Throw ball

Mark a line on the floor with a piece of wool. Throw screwed-up paper balls into a propped-up box from behind the line.

Nodding elephant

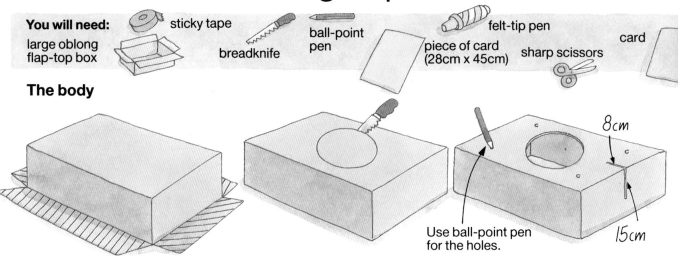

You will need:
large oblong
flap-top box
sticky tape
breadknife
ball-point
pen
piece of card
(28cm x 45cm)
felt-tip pen
sharp scissors
card

The body

Use ball-point pen
for the holes.

8cm

15cm

Turn the box over and
cut off the flaps with a
breadknife.

Cut a circle in the
centre top, large
enough to fit round
your child's waist.

Cut a slit along the top
and down the front, as
shown. Poke four holes
in the top for straps.

The head

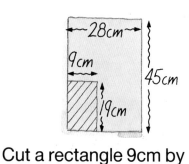

28cm

9cm

19cm

45cm

Cut a rectangle 9cm by
19cm from the corner
of a large piece of
card.

Cut out
this part.

Round off the corners
with scissors. Draw in
a trunk and cut it out.

Draw round the end of
a kitchen-roll tube to
make two circles, as
shown above.

Cut slits from the
centres to very slightly
beyond the edges.

Push the kitchen-roll
tube through the top
hole to make handles.

Tape on two
cardboard
egg box
sections for
eyes.

Cut two tusks out of
the cardboard-box
flaps and glue them
onto the head.

92

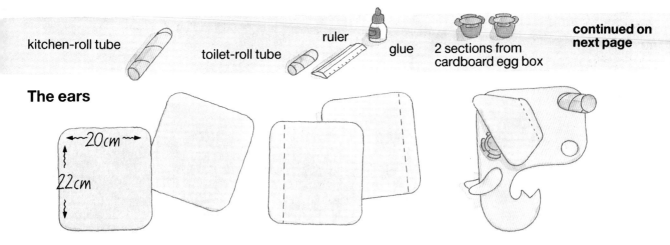

kitchen-roll tube   toilet-roll tube   ruler   glue   2 sections from cardboard egg box

continued on next page

The ears

←20cm→

22cm

Cut two rectangles out of card. Round off the corners, using scissors.

Make a fold down one long side of each rectangle, 4cm from the edge.

Put some glue along the folds and stick the ears onto each side of the head between the eye and the handle.

Joining the head and body

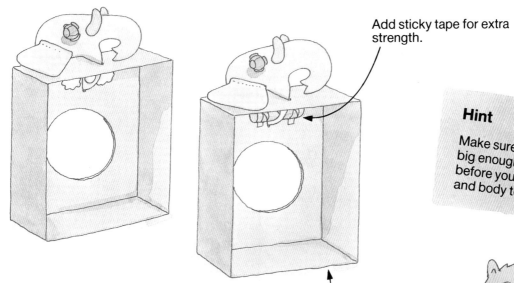

Add sticky tape for extra strength.

Stand the box on end while you fix the head.

Hint

Make sure the hole is big enough for the tube before you fix the head and body together.

Put plenty of glue on either side of the front slit of the body box, on the inside of the box.
   Push the head through the slit from the outside, so that the hole in the head is on the inside.

Push a toilet-roll tube through the hole and press it firmly against the glued area.

93

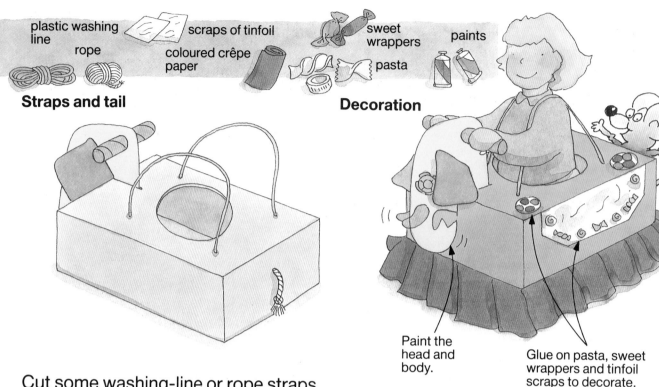

plastic washing line

rope

scraps of tinfoil

coloured crêpe paper

sweet wrappers

pasta

paints

Straps and tail

Decoration

Paint the head and body.

Glue on pasta, sweet wrappers and tinfoil scraps to decorate.

Cut some washing-line or rope straps the right length to fit over the wearer's shoulders. Thread them through the holes and knot them inside.

Make a hole for a tail with a ball-point pen. Thread some rope through and knot it inside. Knot and fray the end.

Cut a strip of crêpe paper about 20cm wide to go round the lower edge of the elephant's body. Attach it with sticky tape. Stretch the lower edge between your hands to make a frilled effect.

Other ideas to try

Dinosaur

Duck

Clown horse

Crêpe-paper mane

Slit crêpe-paper fringe

Spines cut from crêpe-paper.

Paper wings and tail

Yellow socks

Parents' notes

On this page and the following one you will find some general advice about the equipment and materials needed for the projects in this book, and ways of handling them. The specific things you will need for each project are listed at the top of each page. It is a good idea to collect them all together before you start work.

Work with your child, explaining each stage of your project as you set about it, referring to the pictures and discussing the materials. The process of making the things is just as important as the end result. There will be parts of some of the projects that are too difficult or dangerous for children to do themselves, but they can still learn a lot from watching and helping you.

Some of the projects towards the end of the book will take a little longer than the earlier ones. You will probably want to do them in two or three sessions, rather than all at once. Explain this to your child before you start.

Basic equipment

For nearly all the projects you will need the following:

- Scissors – for cutting paper and thin cardboard. Round-ended with metal blades for children and, occasionally, sharp-ended for adults only.

- Knife – for cutting thick cardboard. The best type to use is a breadknife or other sturdy knife with a serrated edge. For adults only.

- Felt-tip pen – for marking lines to cut along.

- Ball-point pen – for making holes in cardboard.

- Ruler – for measuring.

- Pencil

- Glue

- Sticky tape

Finding your materials

You can collect nearly all of the materials you will need by saving the packaging from your everyday shopping. The lists below will help you to spot the sort of things that will come in handy.

Cardboard boxes and cartons for:

cereal (a good source of thin card)

tea bags and loose tea

soap

soap powder

toothpaste tubes

sardines

eggs

biscuits

matches

shoes

milk and juice

pizzas

Plastic containers for:

shampoos and conditioners

fizzy drinks and squashes

yoghurt

margarine

spreads

ice cream

clothes-washing liquid

dishwashing liquid

Polystyrene:

food trays   pizza bases

Lids and caps (metal or plastic) for:

bottles (flat and screw-topped)

jam-jars

toothpaste tubes

margarine and yoghurt tubs

liquid soaps

Cardboard tubes for:

toilet paper

kitchen roll

wrapping paper

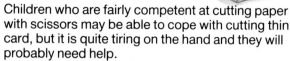

It is also worth saving a few other everyday odds and ends:

Paper:

wrapping paper from flowers or presents

left-over wallpaper

old magazines

sweet wrappers

tissue paper

crêpe paper

Things for tying and threading:

laces

wool

string

rope

plastic washing line

Things from your kitchen

kitchen paper

tinfoil

clingfilm (use microwave clingfilm if possible – it is thicker and less fly-away)

disposable cleaning cloths

thin mopping-up sponges

paper and plastic plates and cups

straws

Asking at shops

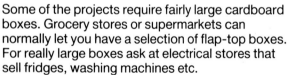

Some of the projects require fairly large cardboard boxes. Grocery stores or supermarkets can normally let you have a selection of flap-top boxes. For really large boxes ask at electrical stores that sell fridges, washing machines etc.

Shoe shops usually have some unwanted, empty shoe boxes and sweet shops may be able to give you large, empty, plastic jars.

Cleaning your materials

Wash things like yoghurt pots and bottle caps before using them and wipe paper plates with a damp cloth. Make sure anything you use is thoroughly dry, however, before using glue or sticky tape on it.

It is a good idea to sterilize some things before use e.g. polystyrene food trays, which are porous and may have held meat. Buy a sterilizing solution from a chemist's and follow the instructions. Then, rinse and dry thoroughly before use.

Cutting cardboard

Children who are fairly competent at cutting paper with scissors may be able to cope with cutting thin card, but it is quite tiring on the hand and they will probably need help.

The best way of cutting thick card and large boxes is to use a breadknife as though it were a saw – the downward stroke away from you should have the most pressure. Make it clear to young children that they should not try to do this themselves and keep the knife out of reach. Make sure your child stands well back when you are sawing.

When cutting the top or bottom section off a box, start by sawing across a corner, then insert the blade and continue.

To cut into a flat surface, first insert the point of a ball-point pen to make a small hole for the blade of the knife to fit into.

Turn the box as you cut, so that the area you are cutting is always at the top. This will give you greater control.

Sticking

●Wallpaper paste. This is good for large areas but is not very strong. For safety always use the non-fungicidal kind. You can store left-over paste in the fridge, covered with clingfilm.

●PVA (polyvinyl acetate) glues. These are also good for large areas. They are available from large newsagent's. Apply the glue with a brush. It is white but dries transparent. Protect clothing and wash brushes after use.

●Strong glue. For some jobs, such as sticking yoghurt pots or bottle caps onto cardboard, you need to use a fairly strong glue. Buy a tube of non-toxic glue from a newsagent. Do not use solvent-based or instant-bond glues.

●Coloured sticky tape. This is good for decoration if you want stripes, bars or criss-cross patterns.

Painting

Use powder paints or liquid poster paints. Powder paint is cheaper but tends to be thinner. You can thicken it by mixing it with wallpaper paste, flour and water paste, PVA glue or soapflakes. If you mix a little washing-up liquid into the paint, it will wash off furniture and clothes more easily. For painting large areas, use small adult-sized brushes.

KITCHEN FUN

This book provides parents and children with lots of easy, tasty and original ideas for things to cook together. There are sweets and savouries, including recipes for everyday dishes or for special occasions. Besides introducing children to some of the most basic cooking techniques and giving them fun and satisfaction, the activities in this book will also help to develop their ideas about size, shape, weight, measurement and time, broaden their vocabulary and give them early counting and reading opportunities.

Juicy jellies

You will need:
3 jellies
1 green
1 yellow
1 other
ready roll icing

  food colouring

flower sweets

angelica

fresh or canned fruit

squirty cream

Jelly pond

Make up green and yellow jellies together, as directed on the packet, in a large mixing bowl. When cool refrigerate until beginning to set.

Cut pieces of icing off the block and colour them by rolling them in a few drops of food colouring. Leave some white.

Make fish, snakes and snails from the icing (see below). Press them firmly onto the inside of a glass or plastic bowl.

When the jelly is nearly set, pour it carefully into the glass bowl.*

Reeds made from angelica pressed into strips of icing.

Weeds made from green icing squeezed through a garlic press.

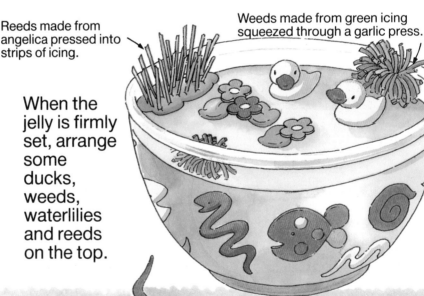

When the jelly is firmly set, arrange some ducks, weeds, waterlilies and reeds on the top.

Fish
Flatten a piece of icing. Cut out body and tail shapes. Press in an eye with a pencil covered in clingfilm. Press on some tiny spots.

Snakes
Roll long sausage shapes and press in eyes.

Ducks
Press two balls together, then pinch out a tail and add a beak.

Waterlilies
Flatten balls and shape them into leaves. Mark with a knife. Place flower sweets on top.

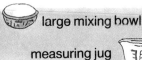 large mixing bowl

 measuring jug

 large, clear, glass or plastic bowl

 wooden spoon

plastic knife

garlic press

 plastic tumblers saucers

pencil covered with clingfilm

Jelly wobblers

Make up a jelly with 75 ml less water than given in the instructions. Allow to cool but not set.

Peel, slice and de-seed fresh fruit, or drain canned fruit, and arrange in plastic tumblers.

Pour on the jelly and leave it to set in the fridge.

When they have set, ease round the sides of the jellies with a plastic knife.

Turn them out onto saucers and decorate the tops with cream and fruit.

Other ideas to try:

Monster in a lake
Roll a long, fat snake out of ready roll icing. Cut it into four sections.

Jelly diamond sweets

Bend the middle sections and place them on a set jelly.

Water babies
On a set jelly, arrange some icing "rocks" and stand jelly babies on them.
Add squirty cream for waves.

*Hint
Don't pour liquid jelly over icing or it will start to dissolve.

Fishy puffs

You will need:

packet of puff pastry (thawed) · 1 egg · lemon · parsley · flour · smoked mackerel or drained can of tuna

Press in lines.

Roll out the puff pastry thinly (about 2 mm deep) on a floured surface.

To make large fish cut round a side plate with a knife. For small fish use scone-cutters.

From the leftover pastry cut out tail shapes with a knife. Use a pen-top dipped in flour to cut out "spots".

Fat bunnies

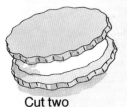

Use scone-cutters to make two circles. Put some filling on one circle and press the other circle over it.

Cut two fat cheeks with a bottle-top. Stick them on.

From another circle cut out two ears.

Roll a small ball for a nose and press out some eyes with a straw. Brush with egg and bake as for fishy puffs.

Leave the edges uncovered.

Place the pastry circle on an oiled baking tray. Brush the edges with beaten egg.

Put some fish on one half of the pastry. Add a squeeze of lemon and some parsley.

Fillings
• Cottage cheese with peas or honey.
• Triangle of processed cheese with a small slice of ham.

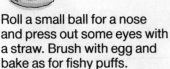

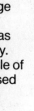

rolling pin · plastic knife, fork and spoon · side plate · large pen-top · straw · scone-cutter · bottle-top · fish-slice · pastry brush · oiled baking tray · cooling rack

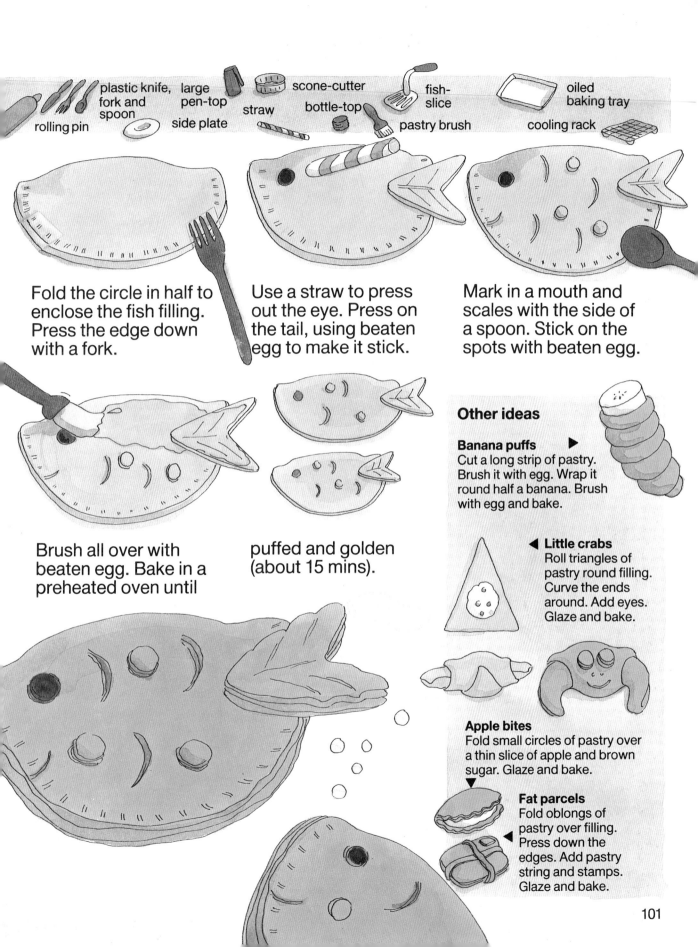

Fold the circle in half to enclose the fish filling. Press the edge down with a fork.

Use a straw to press out the eye. Press on the tail, using beaten egg to make it stick.

Mark in a mouth and scales with the side of a spoon. Stick on the spots with beaten egg.

Brush all over with beaten egg. Bake in a preheated oven until

puffed and golden (about 15 mins).

Other ideas

Banana puffs ▶
Cut a long strip of pastry. Brush it with egg. Wrap it round half a banana. Brush with egg and bake.

◀ **Little crabs**
Roll triangles of pastry round filling. Curve the ends around. Add eyes. Glaze and bake.

Apple bites
Fold small circles of pastry over a thin slice of apple and brown sugar. Glaze and bake.

Fat parcels
Fold oblongs of pastry over filling. Press down the edges. Add pastry string and stamps. Glaze and bake.

101

Valentine tarts

You will need: 100 g plain or self-raising flour · pinch of salt · 25 g margarine · 25 g lard · jam

2 tablespoons cold water · large mixing bowl · plastic scone cutter · knife · teaspoon · plastic bottle-top · cooling rack · greased bun tray

Mix the flour and salt in a large bowl. Cut up the fat and gently rub it in.

Stir in the water quickly with a knife.

Push the dough together with your fingers.

Push in top edge, using clingfilm covered pencil.

Pinch lower edge into a point.

Flatten out gently with fingertips.

Roll out the dough on a floured board until it is about 3 mm thick. Cut out large circles with a scone cutter.

From the scraps cut out some small circles with a bottle-top and make them into hearts as shown.

Bake for about 15 minutes in a preheated oven.

Press the large circles gently into a greased bun tray. Put a large teaspoon of jam in each one and place the hearts on top.

Hints

- Use a ball of dough to press the circles of pastry gently into the bun tray.

- Do not put too much jam in the tarts, or it may bubble over the edges.

- Allow the jam plenty of time to cool down, before touching or tasting the tarts.

Duck on a lake cake

You will need: 1 quantity Victoria sponge cake mix (see page 128). pink and green food colouring jam  icing sugar

 1 large bowl / 2 small bowls / 2 dessert spoons / greased cake tin (approx. 18 cm) 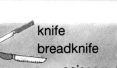 knife / breadknife / scissors / thick felt-tip pen / greaseproof paper sieve / cooling rack

Make up your cake mixture in a large bowl (see page 128).

Put a third of the mixture into each small bowl. Leave a third in the large bowl.

Leave one bowl uncoloured.

Add pink food colouring to one bowl and green colouring to another and mix in well.

Put the three parts of the mixture in separate heaps in a cake tin.

Marble it by dragging a spoon gently through the colours.

Bake in the oven for 40 to 45 minutes.

When it is cool slice it in half with a breadknife and spread one half with jam.

You need this part.

To sift the icing sugar tap the sieve gently with the flat of your hand.

Hint
If the greaseproof paper stencil will not lie flat on the cake, brush it with a little water.

Using the cake tin as a guide to size, draw a simple duck design with a felt-tip pen on greaseproof paper. Cut it out carefully to make a stencil.

Lay the stencil over the cake. Sift icing sugar thickly over it. Lift the paper off carefully.

Jelly baby fun

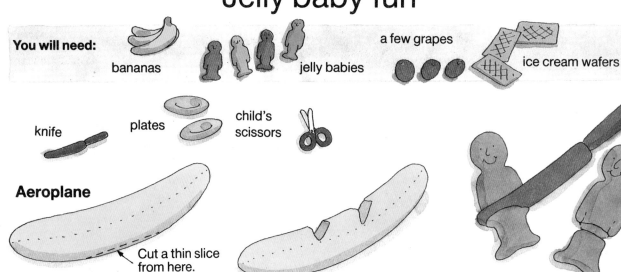

You will need: bananas, jelly babies, a few grapes, ice cream wafers, knife, plates, child's scissors

Aeroplane

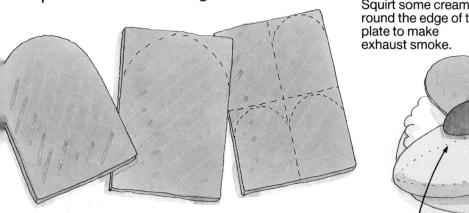

Cut a thin slice from here.

Peel a long straight banana. Cut a thin slice from one side to prevent it from rolling.

Cut two V-shaped sections from the top to make a cockpit.

Cut two jelly babies in half to make a pilot and a co-pilot.

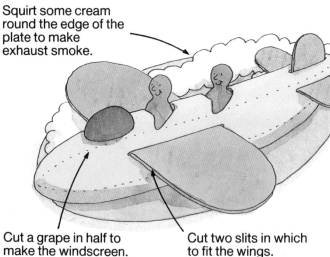

Trim ice cream wafers with scissors to make wings and fins.

Squirt some cream round the edge of the plate to make exhaust smoke.

Cut a grape in half to make the windscreen.

Cut two slits in which to fit the wings.

Other ideas

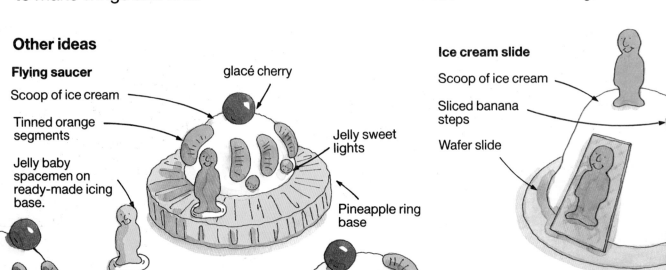

Flying saucer

Scoop of ice cream

Tinned orange segments

Jelly baby spacemen on ready-made icing base.

glacé cherry

Jelly sweet lights

Pineapple ring base

Ice cream slide

Scoop of ice cream

Sliced banana steps

Wafer slide

squirty cream

jelly sweets

jam

Add a quarter of a grape for the windscreen.

Stick on with jam.

Jelly sweet hub caps.

Racing car

Place half a peeled banana on a plate. From the other half cut a slice to place behind it.

Cut a V-shaped seat for the driver. Put the top half of a jelly baby in the seat.

Make wheels from slices cut across the spare half of banana.

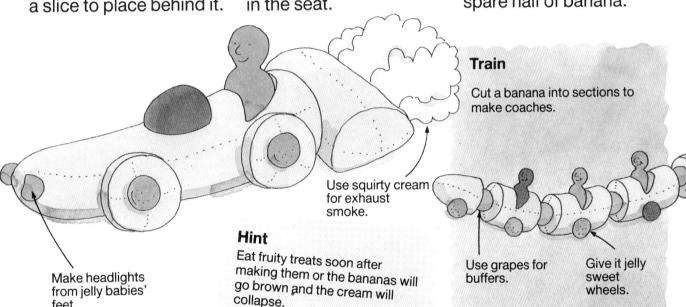

Train

Cut a banana into sections to make coaches.

Use squirty cream for exhaust smoke.

Hint

Eat fruity treats soon after making them or the bananas will go brown and the cream will collapse.

Make headlights from jelly babies' feet.

Use grapes for buffers.

Give it jelly sweet wheels.

Speedboat

A quarter of a banana, flat side up.

A quarter of a grape

Chopped green jelly sea.

Squirty cream

Baby in a blanket

Colour a small piece of ready-roll icing with a few drops of food colouring. Flatten it with your hand to make a "blanket".

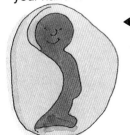

◄ Lay the baby on the blanket and wrap up as shown. Allow to harden.

Flowery hats

You will need: 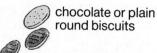 chocolate or plain round biscuits packet chocolate teacakes (marshmallow biscuits) 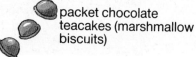 cold water icing sugar jelly diamonds sugar flowers

 small bowl teaspoon large plate knife

Make it quite thick so it doesn't run.

Add a little water to icing sugar to make icing "glue".

Spread a little on the centre of each flat biscuit.

Press teacakes gently onto the centre of the biscuits.

Add flowers and jelly diamond "leaves" round the crown. Stick them on with icing glue. Leave to dry.

Add a ready-roll icing "ribbon" if you like.

Other ideas

Christmas puddings

Spread a biscuit with coloured icing to make a plate.

Stick a teacake on.

Dribble a little white icing "brandy sauce" over the top.

Add small pieces of jelly diamonds for leaves and holly berries.

Flying saucers

Ice a biscuit. Add a teacake. Sprinkle hundreds and thousands around the edge. Add jelly sweet lights.

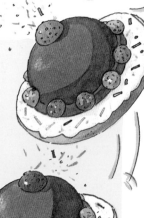

Set oven to:
190°C 375°F
Gas mark 5

Bow-tie bears

You will need:

 150 g self-raising flour

 15 g drinking chocolate

sultanas

ready-roll icing

100 g margarine

50 g castor sugar

 ½ tsp. lemon or vanilla essence

food colouring

icing glue (see opposite page)

greased baking tray

electric food mixer

fish-slice

cooling rack

small bowl

rolling-pin

knife

Put one part back in the mixer with drinking chocolate and blend.

Divide each of the other three parts into three to make nine equal balls.

Combine margarine, flour, sugar and lemon essence in a mixer to make a smooth dough.

Remove the dough and cut it into four equal parts.

From the remaining ball roll eight small balls for noses. Flatten them and add to the centre of each face.

Flatten balls of chocolate dough onto the faces to make ears.

Add sultanas for eyes and one for nose.

Hints

- Space the biscuits well, as the mixture spreads on cooking.

- If the dough is too crumbly after adding chocolate, add a few drops of milk to bind.

- If you have no food mixer, cream the fat and sugar together, then add the flour. Then continue as above.

For the bears' faces flatten eight of the balls onto the baking tray with the palm of your hand.

Bake for 12 to 15 minutes in a preheated oven. Allow to cool in the tin for one minute before removing with fish-slice to cool on rack.

Add a bow-tie when cool.

Bow-ties

Put a few drops of food colouring in a bowl. Knead in ready-roll icing.

Roll it out. Cut oblongs and pinch in the centre, as shown. Stick on with icing "glue".

Cheesy scones

You will need: 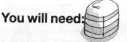 pinch of salt

225 g self-raising flour

 40 g margarine

 150 ml milk

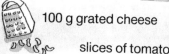 100 g grated cheese

 slices of tomato

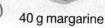 sieve

large bowl

rolling-pin

knife

scone-cutter (5 cm)

greased baking tray

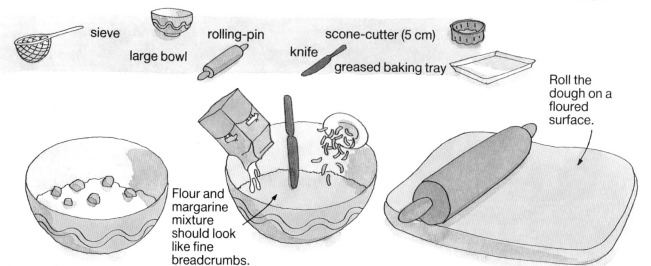

Flour and margarine mixture should look like fine breadcrumbs.

Roll the dough on a floured surface.

Sift flour and salt into large bowl. Cut the margarine up and rub it lightly into the flour.

Stir in half the grated cheese. Add the milk and stir quickly with a knife to mix it in.

Push the dough gently together into a ball. Roll it out until it is about 2 cm thick.

Cut out circles with a scone-cutter. Put them on a greased baking sheet.

Sprinkle the rest of the cheese on top and bake for 10 minutes in the preheated oven.

Cut them in half. Fill with sliced tomatoes.

Cheesy twists   **Oven:**   190°C   375°F   Gas mark 5

Roll out some shortcrust pastry thinly. Spread half of it with yeast extract and sprinkle cheese on top.
Fold the other half over the top of the filling.

Cut into strips, twist once, and lay on a greased baking tray.

Bake in a preheated oven for 10 to 15 minutes.

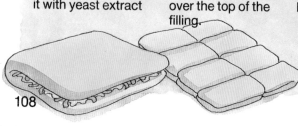

Hints

●Don't handle the dough too much, or it will become tough.

●If the oven is not hot enough the scones may not rise well.

108

Rice rabbit

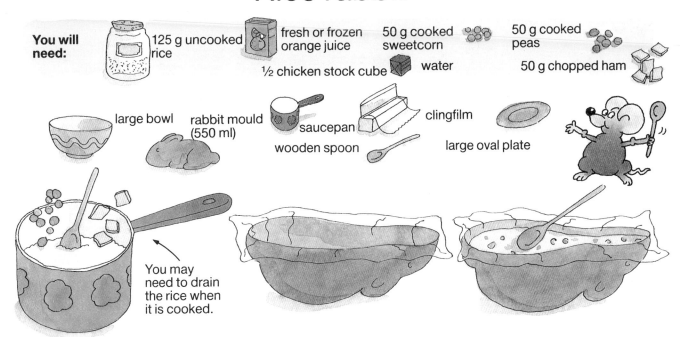

You will need: 125 g uncooked rice · fresh or frozen orange juice · 50 g cooked sweetcorn · 50 g cooked peas · ½ chicken stock cube · water · 50 g chopped ham

large bowl · rabbit mould (550 ml) · saucepan · wooden spoon · clingfilm · large oval plate

You may need to drain the rice when it is cooked.

Cook the rice as directed on the packet, using half orange juice and half stock as the cooking liquid. Add ham and vegetables.

Line the mould with clingfilm, pressing it well into all the hollows.

Fill the mould with the rice mixture, pressing it firmly down with the back of a wooden spoon.

Put the plate over the mould and then turn both the right way up.

Hints

● Make sure the rice is pressed firmly into ears, nose and tail before filling the rest of the mould.

● You could use cooked celery or broccoli instead of sweetcorn and peas.

Serve with carrot sticks in a section of hollowed out cucumber.

Use shredded lettuce for grass.

Lift the mould off and carefully peel off the clingfilm. Eat warm or cold.

Christmas tree

You will need:

mild ginger biscuit dough (see page 128)

solid boiled sweets in assorted colours

flour

rolling-pin

non-stick baking parchment

greaseproof paper

felt-tip pen

flat baking tray

scissors

knife

plastic bottle-top or child's small pastry cutters

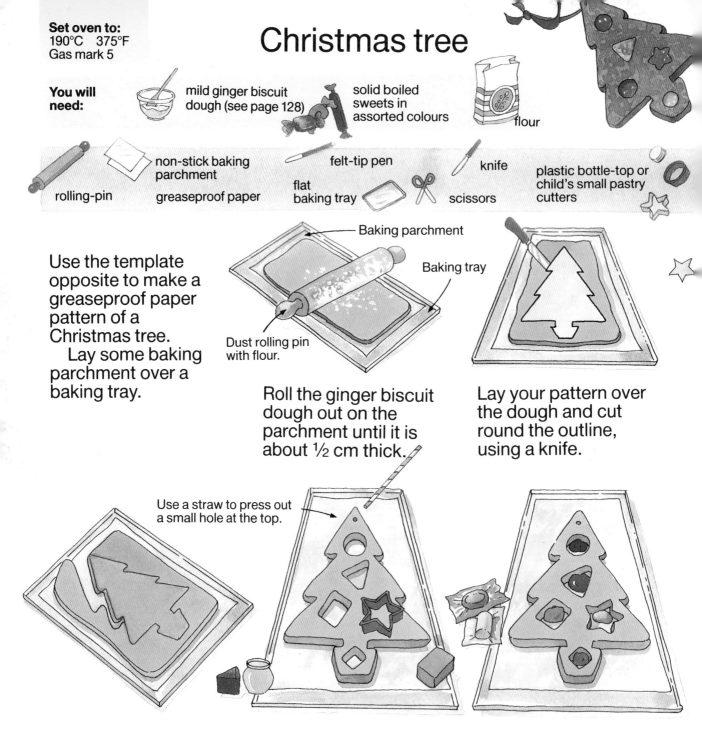

Baking parchment

Baking tray

Dust rolling pin with flour.

Use the template opposite to make a greaseproof paper pattern of a Christmas tree.

Lay some baking parchment over a baking tray.

Roll the ginger biscuit dough out on the parchment until it is about ½ cm thick.

Lay your pattern over the dough and cut round the outline, using a knife.

Use a straw to press out a small hole at the top.

Lift the pattern off and carefully peel away the dough from the edges.

Cut shapes out of the dough tree, using a bottle-top or child's pastry cutters.

Bake in a preheated oven for 10 minutes. Take it out of the oven, place a boiled sweet in each cut-out shape and bake for a further five minutes.

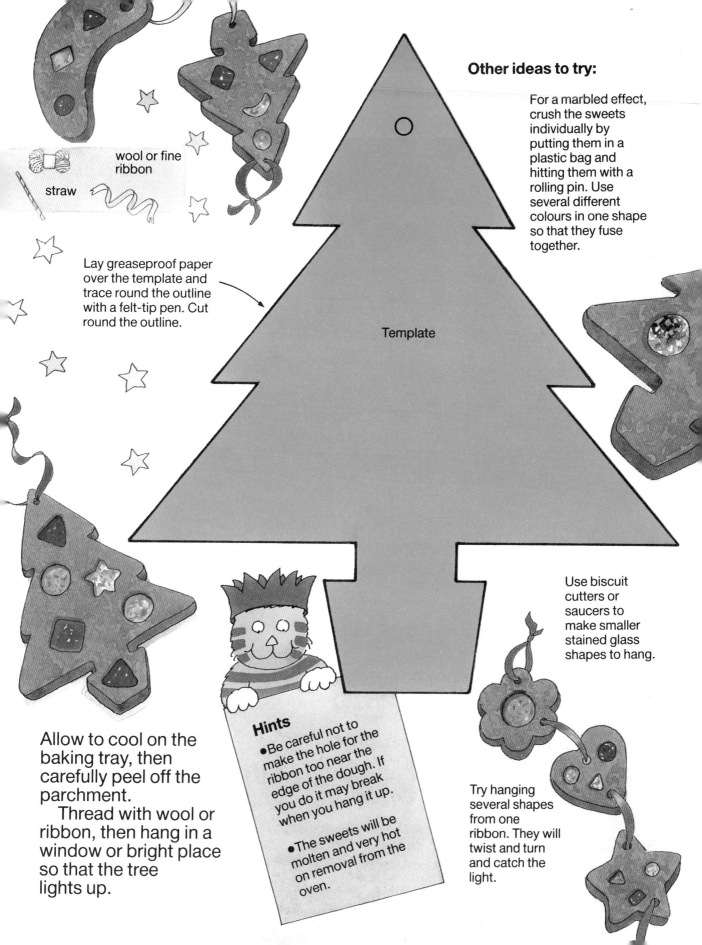

Other ideas to try:

For a marbled effect, crush the sweets individually by putting them in a plastic bag and hitting them with a rolling pin. Use several different colours in one shape so that they fuse together.

wool or fine ribbon

straw

Lay greaseproof paper over the template and trace round the outline with a felt-tip pen. Cut round the outline.

Template

Use biscuit cutters or saucers to make smaller stained glass shapes to hang.

Allow to cool on the baking tray, then carefully peel off the parchment.

Thread with wool or ribbon, then hang in a window or bright place so that the tree lights up.

Hints
● Be careful not to make the hole for the ribbon too near the edge of the dough. If you do it may break when you hang it up.

● The sweets will be molten and very hot on removal from the oven.

Try hanging several shapes from one ribbon. They will twist and turn and catch the light.

Cress creatures

You will need: cress seeds   jug of cold water brown or black felt or paper   scissors

 potatoes   dinner plate   scrap of white felt or paper

Woolly sheep

Tease some cotton wool into a rough oblong shape for the body and lay it on a plate.

Cut some ears, a face and some legs out of black felt and lay them on the cotton wool.

Cut the eyes out of white felt and mark in the centre with a felt-tip pen.

Don't sprinkle the seeds too thickly.

Add some extra cotton wool for the forehead and tail.

Water cotton wool thoroughly.

Sprinkle some cress seeds over the cotton wool.

Keep the cotton wool moist by pouring a little water onto the plate each day.

In a few days the sheep's fleece will be ready to shear with scissors and eat.

Ideas for eating your cress

With cottage cheese or cream cheese in sandwiches.

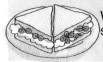
With egg in sandwiches.

As a garnish for sliced tomatoes or cucumbers.

As a filling in hot buttered scones (see page 108).

As a topping for baked potatoes with cream cheese or chopped grilled bacon.

cotton wool — black felt-tip pen — carrot — potato peeler

Hairy caterpillar

Cut some bits of carrot to fit in the eyes, nose and mouth.

Scrub some potatoes. Choose a small one for the head and cut out a face with a potato peeler.

Slice the tops off the other potatoes. Scoop some of the potato out and replace it with cotton wool.

Water the cotton wool and sprinkle it with seeds.

Arrange the potatoes in order of size behind the head. Watch the caterpillar get hairier and hairier.

Clown

Cut a slice from the base of a potato so it will stand. Cut out a face and insert a carrot-stick nose. Grow some hair on top.

Add pieces of potatoe for feet.

Other ideas to try:

Lion
Use orange felt and a frayed wool tail. Give him a cotton wool mane.

Stencils
Place a shaped biscuit cutter on cotton wool. Sprinkle seeds evenly inside them carefully remove cutter.

Names

Tease some cotton wool into fat strings and arrange in letter shapes on a plate.

Hedgehog
Find a potato with a pointed end for a nose. Cut out some eyes. Grow prickles on his back.

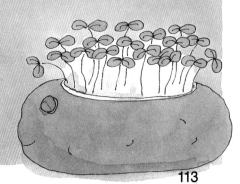

Hallowe'en lantern

You will need:

large, ripe melon

orange crêpe paper

old newspaper

dessertspoon

two bowls

sharp knife*

kitchen roll

string

potato peeler

small torch

Newspaper will stop your working surface from getting sticky.

Spread out some newspaper and put the melon on it. Slice off the most pointed end with a sharp knife.

Scoop the seeds out into a bowl. Scoop the flesh from the melon and the lid into another bowl, leaving a shell about 1 cm thick.

Cut out some eyes, a nose and a mouth, using a sharp knife.* Make some holes to thread a string handle through, using a potato peeler.

Turn the melon upside down and allow to drain for a few minutes. Use kitchen towel to pat the inside as dry as possible.

Line the inside with crêpe paper, covering the cut out shapes and pressing it against the sides. Thread string through the holes.

Switch on a small torch. Place it inside the melon, so the light shines through the crêpe paper. Put the lid on.

114   *For safety you could put a cork on the end when not in use.*

Easter nests

You will need: 60 g margarine ½ small beaten egg food colouring

 125 g flour 60 g sugar mixed spice ready-roll icing or white marzipan

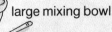 large mixing bowl  sieve 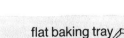 rolling pin flat baking tray wooden spoon garlic press 6cm scone cutter plate

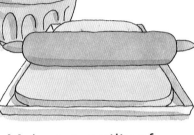

Make a quantity of biscuit dough*. Roll out ½cm thick on a flat baking tray.

Cut 6 rounds, evenly spaced with a 6cm scone cutter. Remove the excess dough very carefully.

Squeeze the excess dough through a garlic press. Catch the strings of dough on a plate.

Lay twisted strings of dough round the edges of your rounds to make nests.

Bake for 15-17 minutes in a pre-heated oven until golden.

You could buy candy or chocolate eggs to fill your nests.

When cool, fill with eggs made from marzipan or icing with a little food colouring kneaded into it.

*See page 128 for recipe, substituting mixed spice for ginger.

Giant stripey bees

You will need:

 1 plain swiss roll

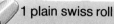 1 chocolate swiss roll

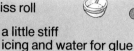 a little stiff icing and water for glue

chocolate buttons

small coloured chocolate sweets

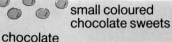

rice paper or greaseproof paper

pencil

large plate

scissors

knife

green paper

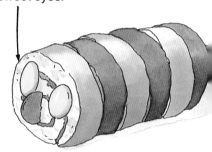

Stick on chocolate sweet eyes.

Divide each swiss roll into three, then divide each third into three to make nine slices per cake.

Each bee will need three slices from each cake. Sandwich alternate colours together with icing and water "glue."

Press a chocolate button sideways into each end for a nose and tail.

For a party you could decorate the plate with green paper leaves.

Draw and cut a pair of wings from folded paper.

Ease spaces between the second and third slices with a knife to insert wings. Arrange bees on a large plate.

Other ideas to try:

Owl

Turn a slice on its end for the head.

Use half slices for the wings.

Use jelly diamonds for ears, beak and feet.

Butterfly

Decorate the wings with coloured sweets and jelly diamonds.

You could make the owl and the butterfly with only one colour of cake.

Pink sunset pudding

You will need: grated rind and juice of 2 lemons | red food colouring

1 tin condensed milk (400 ml)

2 eggs, separated

100 g castor sugar

2 large bowls | tin opener | electric whisk | wooden spoon | large metal spoon | ovenproof flan dish (approx. 23 cm) | knife

Mix together the lemon juice and rind, egg yolks, condensed milk and a few drops of red food colouring.

In another bowl whisk the egg whites with a few drops of food colouring until stiff.

Whisk in half the sugar, then fold in the remaining sugar using a metal spoon.

Pour the milk mixture into a flan dish. Spoon the egg whites on top.

Flick into swirls and peaks using the knife.

Hints

● Make sure the bowl for the egg whites is dry and completely free of grease.

● This pudding tastes even better the day after you have made it.

● It can be used as a filling in a shortcrust pastry case, which has been baked blind for 10 minutes.

Bake for 12 to 15 minutes until crisp and lightly browned. Eat warm or cold.

Ham, cheese and pineapple slices

You will need:

 butter for spreading

4 tinned pineapple rings

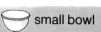 4 slices processed cheese

4 slices thin-cut ham

4 small slices of bread

butterfly-type tin opener

kitchen roll

small bowl

butter knife

fish-slice

Press firmly on the bottom of the tin.

Open the tin and pour off any syrup into a bowl.

Use kitchen roll to pat the pineapple dry.

Using the tin as a cutter, press out four circles each from the bread, ham and cheese slices.

Toast the bread lightly on both sides under a grill, then butter it on one side.

Put a circle of ham, then pineapple on each round of bread, then top with cheese.

Using a fish-slice replace under the grill and heat until the cheese is melted and bubbling.

Hint

Use up any scraps of bread to make breadcrumbs in a blender. Use them for a savoury crumble topping or stuffing, or freeze them for later use.

Pretend pizzas

Toast some circles of bread, as above. Spread with a little tomato paste.

Sprinkle sliced vegetables and scraps of ham, salami or tuna on top.

Top with cheese and sprinkle sparingly with dried herbs. Place under the grill.

Hedgehog nibbles

You will need: a little milk • carrot sticks • cucumber slices • cream cheese • crisps • savoury stick biscuits • sultanas

large plate • wooden spoon • bowl • tea-towel

Rest the bowl on a tea-towel to prevent it slipping.

Beat the cream cheese with a little milk to soften it.

Put the cheese on a plate and pat it into a pear-shape with the wooden spoon.

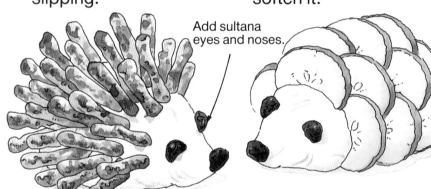

Add sultana eyes and noses.

Press in vegetables, crisps, or savoury stick biscuits to make the hedgehog's prickles.

Hints

• You can make pink hedgehogs by adding a little tomato ketchup to the cheese.

• Try sweet hedgehogs, using pieces of tinned or fresh fruit for prickles.

Faces

Use a selection of sliced, shredded or chopped vegetables to create faces on bread circles (or rolls cut in half) spread with butter or cheese spread.

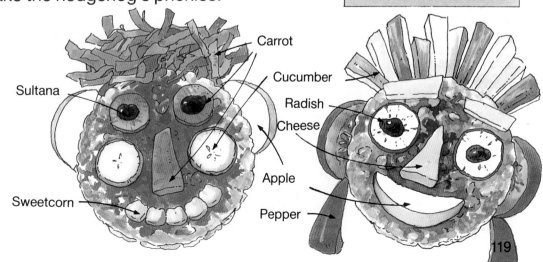

Sultana

Sweetcorn

Carrot

Cucumber

Radish

Cheese

Apple

Pepper

Dreamy drinks

Milk shakes

Whisk the ingredients together in a tall jug, using a hand whisk. Or use an electric blender, but don't remove the lid until the machine has completely stopped.

Use wide straws for thick shakes. If you want thinner shakes reduce the amount of ice cream and add ice cubes.

The amounts given will make enough for one adult and two children.

Vanilla

Top with squirty cream and a glacé cherry.

Chocolate

Top with squirty cream and grated chocolate or chocolate vermicelli.

Hint

Save the juice from cans of fruit to make refreshing drinks. Dilute with water, fruit juices or lemonade.

You will need:

300 ml milk

4 tablespoons vanilla ice cream

¼ teaspoon vanilla essence

300 ml milk

4 tablespoons chocolate ice cream

1 tablespoon chocolate dessert syrup

Other ideas to try:

Orange yoghurt drink

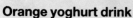

300 ml natural yoghurt

juice of 2 oranges

2 to 3 tablespoons runny honey

Blend together as for milk shakes. Decorate with a slice of orange.

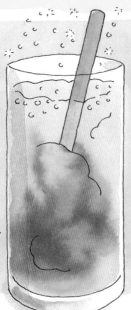

Ice cream soda

Fill a tall glass two thirds full of lemonade, or your favourite fizzy drink.
Add one or two scoops of ice cream and stir with a long spoon.

Strawberry

Top with tinned or sliced fresh strawberries.

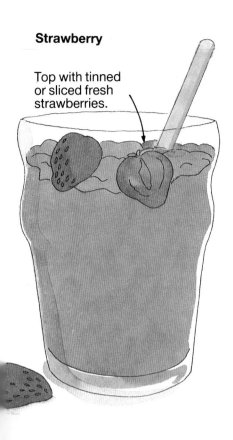

300 ml milk

150 ml strawberry yoghurt

3 tablespoons strawberry ice cream

Blackcurrant

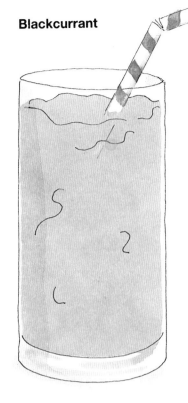

300 ml milk

6 tablespoons vanilla ice cream

3 tablespoons blackcurrant concentrate

Banana

1 ripe banana

300 ml milk

4 tablespoons vanilla ice cream

2 teaspoons honey

Squashy orange

Roll, squeeze and pinch a thin-skinned orange until it feels very soft all over.
Chill it, if you like, then poke a hole near the top with a potato peeler. Insert a short piece of straw and then drink.

Fun with ice cubes

Try freezing pieces of fruit, mint leaves, rose petals in ice to make decorative ice cubes, or freeze fruit juices to liven up drinks of squash.

Microwave castles

You will need:

140 g self-raising flour 75 g butter 1 egg, beaten 1½ tbsp. milk

 ½ tsp. baking-powder   60 g soft brown sugar   ¾ can blackcurrant pie filling   squirty cream

6 paper cups*   wooden spoon   large plate

large bowl   large metal spoon   knife

Stand the cups in a circle on a plate.

Cut up the butter and rub it into the flour and baking powder. Mix in the sugar.

Mix in the egg and milk and half the tin of fruit pie-filling.

Put half a tablespoonful of fruit pie-filling into the bottom of each paper cup.

Fill each cup with the flour mixture until about half full.

Put in a micro-wave** oven. Cook on "high", turning once, for about four minutes. Stand for one minute.

Hint

Use up leftover pie-filling as a hot sauce for ice cream. Heat it in the microwave.

Turn out the castles, then decorate with squirty cream.

*Don't use plastic cups. Some plastics give off dangerous fumes
**Do not use an ordinary oven.

Munchy mice

You will need:
250 g icing sugar
125 g dessicated coconut
pink food colouring
200 ml condensed milk
6 pieces pink wool or red liquorice
flaked almonds
chocolate drops and jelly sweets

wooden spoon
clingfilm
pencil
large bowl
small bowl

Place the pear-shaped bodies on a plate covered with clingfilm.

Mix condensed milk, icing sugar and coconut to a stiff paste in a large bowl. Put half of it in a small bowl.

Pour a few drops of food colouring into the large bowl and mix it in evenly.

Divide the mixture in each bowl into three pieces. Shape each piece into a pear-shaped body.

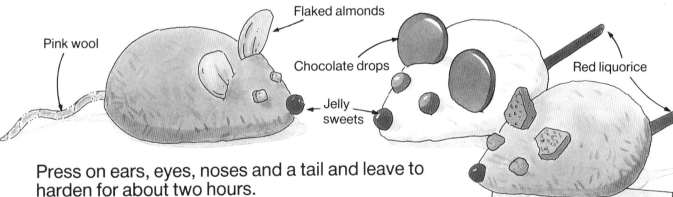

Flaked almonds
Pink wool
Chocolate drops
Jelly sweets
Red liquorice

Press on ears, eyes, noses and a tail and leave to harden for about two hours.

Other ideas to try:

Birthday numbers
Draw a large number on greaseproof paper and cover it with clingfilm.
Use this as a pattern on which to place Munchy Mice mixture.
Press small sweets on top to decorate.

Little sweets
Roll small balls of the mixture and press a sweet onto the top of each one.

Hint

Press holes in which to place ears, eyes, noses and tails with a pencil covered with clingfilm.
This will help them to stick. Or you could use jam or icing sugar and water to glue them in position.

123

Ice cream cake surprise

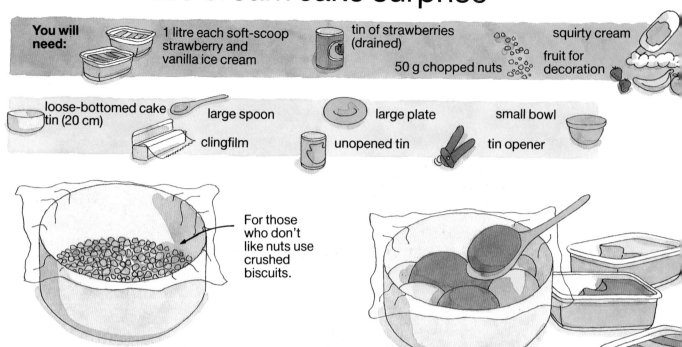

You will need:
- 1 litre each soft-scoop strawberry and vanilla ice cream
- tin of strawberries (drained)
- 50 g chopped nuts
- squirty cream
- fruit for decoration
- loose-bottomed cake tin (20 cm)
- large spoon
- clingfilm
- large plate
- unopened tin
- small bowl
- tin opener

For those who don't like nuts use crushed biscuits.

Line the cake tin with clingfilm. Sprinkle chopped nuts to cover the base.

Cover the nuts with alternate scoops of pink and white ice cream. Press down well.

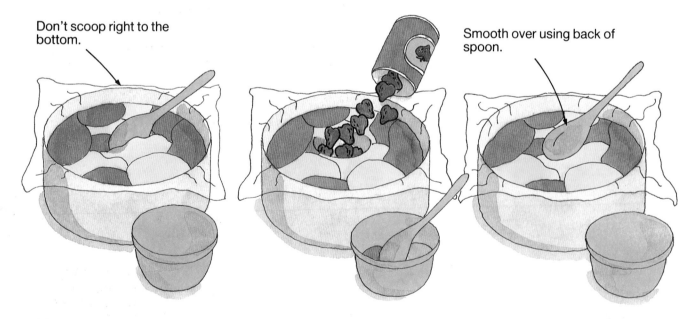

Don't scoop right to the bottom.

Smooth over using back of spoon.

Using a spoon, scoop some ice cream out of the centre into a small bowl.

Pour drained fruit into the hollow, almost to the top.

Replace the scooped out ice cream over the top. Freeze until firm.

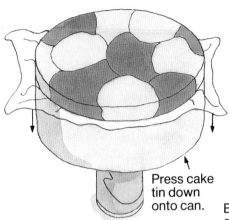

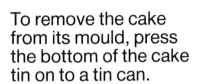

Press cake tin down onto can.

To remove the cake from its mould, press the bottom of the cake tin on to a tin can.

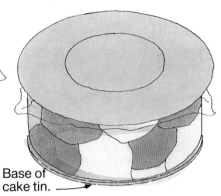

Base of cake tin.

Put a plate on top, turn it over and remove the cake tin base and clingfilm.

Decorate with squirty cream and fruit.

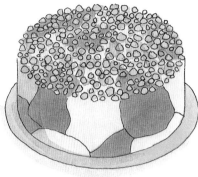

Allow it to soften for about 30 minutes. Cut as required.

Other ideas to try:

Wafer surprise

Lay a slice of ice cream on a wafer. Press into it a selection of the following:

jelly sweets

slices of tinned or fresh fruit

chocolate buttons

Press on a second wafer lid and freeze until firm

Jelly-mould ice creams

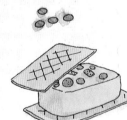

Use small jelly moulds lined with clingfilm as ice cream moulds. Press down firmly into all corners.

Hints

- Use oven gloves when handling frozen tins to avoid freezer burn.

- To cut ice cream use a knife dipped in hot water.

- To get ice cream out of a mould, dip the mould very briefly into hot water.

- You can add crushed meringues to the ice cream if you like.

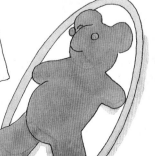

Banana lollies

You will need: firm bananas, runny honey, chopped nuts

new or sterilized lolly sticks, 2 large plates, clingfilm, saucer, knife, pastry brush

Pour some honey into a saucer and nuts onto a plate.

Insert a clean lolly stick into half a peeled banana. Brush it with honey.

Roll the banana in the nuts until it is covered. Sprinkle more over if necessary.

Arrange on a plate covered with clingfilm and then freeze.

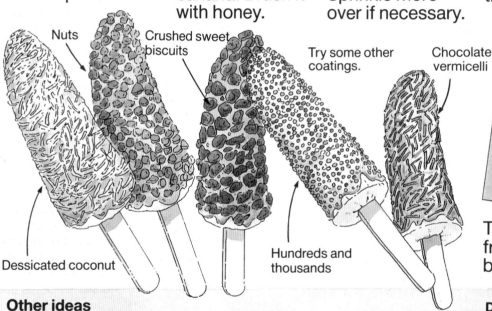

Nuts

Crushed sweet biscuits

Try some other coatings.

Chocolate vermicelli

Dessicated coconut

Hundreds and thousands

Hints

- If the honey is too stiff, warm the jar (without its lid) in the microwave for a few seconds, or in hot water.

- You can use the handle end of plastic spoons if you haven't got any lolly sticks.

Take out of freezer 2 hours before eating.

Other ideas

Yoghurt melties

3 tablespoons frozen orange juice (unthawed)
6 tablespoons natural yoghurt
caster sugar to taste
3 tablespoons water

Mix all the ingredients together until mushy.

Pour into an ice-cube tray or the moulded plastic tray from a chocolate box.

Freeze. Turn out as needed.

Fruit lollies

Freeze fruit squash or the syrup from tinned fruit.

Don't forget to add sticks before freezing.

Drip-free lollies

When quite cool pour liquid jelly into small moulds such as egg cups or ice-cube trays.

Try layers of jelly and cooled custard or banana mashed with strawberry jam.

Parents' notes

Getting prepared

It is worth spending time on careful preparation before you start cooking to make things go smoothly. Get children into good kitchen habits from the start.

● Start by putting on aprons and washing hands.

● Clear a surface so that you have plenty of space to work on and show children how to wipe it down well.

● Gather all the ingredients and utensils before you begin and check them off together from the panels at the top of the pages.

● Prop up this book so that you can see your chosen page carefully. A cook's bookstand is ideal for doing this.

● To make clearing up easier put some old newspapers on the floor.

● If you will need the oven, set it to the right temperature before you begin.

Weighing and measuring

● It is a good idea to spoon dry ingredients onto scales rather than pouring them from a packet. There will be more control and less spillage.

● Instead of scales you could use a measuring jug, which shows levels for dry ingredients as well as liquids.

● Stand jugs and liquids on a tray. Drips and dribbles won't run all over your work area and need immediate clearing up.

● Children can measure spoonfuls of liquid from a bowl rather than pouring from a bottle. Tip measure into a small jug for easy handling.

Utensils

Jugs: Use plastic jugs for measuring or pouring wherever possible. They are safer and light to handle.

Bowls: should always be the right size for the job: egg-whites can quadruple in volume; flour and icing sugar can drift in clouds from a small bowl; china bowls hold steady for mixing and whisking. Small plastic bowls are easy to handle when adding other ingredients.

To avoid slipping stand bowls on a tea towel while creaming and mixing. Small bowls are useful to take discarded egg shells.

Put used cutlery blade end down into mugs.

Knives: Use round-ended knives wherever possible. If you need to use a sharp knife, put a piece of cork on the tip when not in use.

Tinopeners: Use the "butterfly" type if possible – they do not leave a ragged edge on the tin. Wrap lids carefully in double newspaper and discard immediately. To drain the contents of a tin pour slowly into a sieve over a bowl at least as wide.

Cutters: use plastic cutters. Metal ones are sharp and could be pressed into dough upside down by mistake, hurting a child's hand. You can also use plastic tumblers, washed aerosol caps etc. for cutting out shapes.

Wooden spoons: come in different lengths. Choose a short one for a child's use.

Food graters: plastic ones are safer than metal. Grating is quite hard work and children may tire of it quickly. Take over yourself when the item becomes too small to handle safely.

Electrical gadgets

These are great time and effort savers and there is no reason why a small child should not help use them with careful supervision. Never leave an appliance plugged in and unattended. Keep them well away from sinks and bowls of liquid.

Food processors: make sure the machine has completely stopped, before taking off the lid and removing the contents.

Egg whisks: use a high-sided bowl. For safety and to avoid the mixture flying off, switch beaters on and off while blades are inside the bowl.

Ovens

● Make sure that children are well aware of the dangers of a hot oven. Make an obvious show of wearing oven gloves even while just checking baking progress – the door and door knobs on some ovens can become quite hot.
● Ask small children to stand well back from an oven. There could be a blast of hot air in their face and they shouldn't get underfoot while you deal with hot food.
● Check that you have a clear heatproof space ready to take a hot dish before you you open up the oven.
● Use a fish slice for transferring food safely to a cooling rack.
● Some foods need to be cooled in the baking tray but make sure you place them well out of reach.

Freezers

Use oven gloves to avoid freezer burn, especially from metal containers such as cake-tins and ice-cube trays.

Microwave ovens

Be careful to stress that in some cases the container might be cool, but the contents very hot. Paper containers will feel very hot to the touch as the heat of the food comes through.

When using clingfilm in the microwave make sure it is the non-toxic kind especially for microwave use.

Foods

Flour: the recipes in this book use white flour. Other flours can be used, but may require more liquid to achieve the right consistency.

Food colourings: if you are worried about the effect of these additives, you can get non-artificial food colourings from health food stores.

Extend your range of colours by mixing various combinations before adding to the food.

To colour ready-roll icing put a few drops of colouring in a bowl and knead the required amount of icing into it until the colour is even. If the colouring makes the icing too wet, sift a little icing sugar into it and knead it in.

To colour ordinary icing make up the icing slightly stiffer than needed, then add the drops of colour a little at a time until the right colour and consistency is reached.

Mild ginger biscuit dough

125 g plain flour
60 g margarine
60 g brown sugar
½ a small beaten egg
1 tsp ground ginger

● Beat the margarine and sugar together until creamy.
● Add the egg, a little at a time.
● Sift in the flour and ginger.
● Mix well to make a firm dough.
If it is too soft add a little more flour.

Victoria sandwich cake mix

100 g margarine
100 g castor sugar
100 g self-raising flour
2 eggs

● Cream the margarine and sugar together until light and fluffy.
● Beat in the eggs gradually, adding a little flour each time to prevent curdling.
● Fold in the rest of the flour.